Trouble and Turnips

reading basics **plus**

HARPER & ROW, PUBLISHERS *1817*   NEW YORK   HAGERSTOWN   SAN FRANCISCO   LONDON

1977 Printing

CONTRIBUTORS

DOLORES R. AMATO
A. DICKSON CARROLL
CHERIE A. CLODFELTER
LYNETTE SAINE GAINES
ERIC P. HAMP
PHILLIP L. HARRIS
JOSEPH A. LUCERO
MATTIE CLAYBROOK WILLIAMS

Special acknowledgment to Sister Colette Zirbes
and Marilyn Buckley Hanf.

ACKNOWLEDGMENTS

"As my eyes . . ." from *Chippewa Music — II* by Frances Densmore.
Smithsonian Institution, Bureau of American Ethnology, Bulletin 53.
Published by Government Printing Office, Washington, D.C. "At the edge of
the world" from *Singing for Power: The Song Magic of the Papago Indians
of Southern Arizona* by Ruth Murray Underhill. Copyright 1938 by the
Regents of the University of California; renewed © 1966 by Ruth Murray
Underhill. Published by the University of California Press, Berkeley,
California. Reprinted by permission of the Regents of the University of
California.

Big Sister and Little Sister by Charlotte Zolotow. Text copyright © 1966 by
Charlotte Zolotow. Adapted and reprinted by permission of Harper & Row,
Publishers, Inc., New York.

The Case of the Stolen Code Book by Barbara Rinkoff. Illustrated by
Leonard Shortall. Text © 1971 by Barbara Rinkoff. Illustrations © 1971 by
Leonard Shortall. Adapted and reprinted by permission of Crown Publishers,
Inc., New York. *Charley, Charlotte, and the Golden Canary* by Charles
Keeping. Copyright © 1967 by Charles Keeping. Adapted and reprinted by
permission of Franklin Watts, Inc., New York, and Oxford University Press,
London.

EDITORS BRADLEY HANNAN, INGEBORG HEY
ELAINE S. GOLDBERG, DIANE K. LINDEMAN, SYLVIA J. ROSENSTEIN
ELISE C. LEAHY, SYLVIA BACE

DIRECTING EDITORS MARTHA HAYES and EDDY JO BRADLEY

DESIGN BILL NEWTON, DIANE HUTCHINSON, KRISTIN NELSON

ILLUSTRATION BILL and JUDY ANDERSON pages 106-115, 282-294; DENNIS ANDERSON pages 84-94; RAY APP pages 141-154; LOU ARONSON pages 268-278; MARC BALENCHIA pages 95, 162; ROBERT BAUMGARTNER pages 120-128; RON BRADFORD page 200; LORINDA BRYAN CAULEY pages 22-25; DAVID CUNNINGHAM pages 279, 308-309; THOMAS DI GRAZIA pages 28-33; BLAIR DRAWSON pages 57-64; TOM DUNNINGTON pages 155-161; JOHN FAULKNER pages 175-176, 219-220, 295-297; ATI FORBERG pages 68-74; CLAIRE GREGORY page 138; JACK HAESLEY pages 26-27, 39-41, 56; HANDELAN PEDERSEN, INC. pages 310-320; NICOLE HOLLANDER pages 256-265; TRINA SCHART HYMAN pages 201-218; CARL KOCK cover; DORA LEDER pages 184-199; JARED D. LEE pages 42-45; ROBERT MASHERIS pages 9-12, 65-67, 117-119, 181-183, 243-247, 266-267; SUE MASSEY pages 13-21; LARRY MIKEC pages 129-137; TAK MURAKAMI pages 54-55, 75-80; BARBARA PRITZEN pages 34-38; TERRY ROSE pages 177-180; CAROLE SCHUMACHER page 234; BILL SHIRES pages 46-53, 116; ARVIS STEWART pages 235-242; ED TABER pages 81-83, 97-98, 139-140, 298-307; PHERO THOMAS pages 96, 280-281; JOHN WALLNER pages 226-233.

PHOTOGRAPHY BILL BINZEN pages 163-174; RAY ELLIS, RAPHO GUILLUMETTE PICTURES pages 222-225; JAMES MARCHAEL pages 248-255; ROBERT SPEAR pages 99-105.

CONTENTS

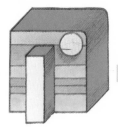

Collection 5

Collection 1

we have   we would   he had   he would

we ha ve   we woul d   he ha d   he woul d

we've   we'd   he'd   he'd

ā	ō	ngk
main	coal	sink
base	soap	sank
tray		drink
vase		blink
		drank

10

Words You Can Read

sail + boat = sailboat

bath + room = bathroom

1. "I am <u>sorry</u>," said Meg after she stepped on my foot.

2. I eat <u>breakfast</u> before I go to school in the morning.

3. I like the <u>kitchen</u> more than any other room because I like the smell of food that is cooking.

4. Jo had <u>dirt</u> all over her after she fell in the mud.

5. A year has 12 <u>months</u>.

6. The chipmunk was <u>hungry</u> because it had not eaten anything all day.

Words You Can Read

entry word

pronunciation

meaning or definition

don key (dong′kē) an animal that looks a little like a horse, but has longer ears and a shorter mane

alphabetical order	glide	search
apart	glossary	second
arroz con pollo	gobble	shortstop
Chippewa	gold	sign
Connecticut	ivy	subway
count	order	swirly
decide	Papago	traveler
doe	potato	tug
donkey	prairie	turnip
edge	quiet	twice
except	restaurant	whole
fact	rose hip tea	wolf

A B C D E

Tempe Wick   by Gerry Jung

Tempe Wick looked out the window. The snow looked beautiful, but Tempe really didn't see it. She was lost in thought. She knew that the little puffs of smoke in the air were from the fires of soldiers. They were now on their own after fighting the British under General George Washington. The soldiers were tired, had no food, and wanted to go home.

Mr. Bright, who lived down the road, had come over one day last week to talk to Tempe and her mother about those soldiers.

"It's a good idea to stay inside, Tempe. And you'd better keep your horse locked in the barn. Those men want to get home badly, and a good horse could get them there! You need that horse to help you with the work around here." That was what Mr. Bright had said.

Tempe's thoughts turned away from the soldiers when her mother called her. "Are you all right, Mother?" Tempe asked. But even as she asked, Tempe knew her mother was not all right. She had been in bed for two days and could hardly eat anything. Her skin felt hot.

"Can't I make you some tea, Mother?" asked Tempe.

Mrs. Wick closed her eyes. "Well, I think I'd better try some," she said softly.

As her mother was sipping the tea, Tempe looked at her and knew she had to do something. "I'm not going to wait any longer, Mother," she said. "I'm going to get something for you from the doctor!"

"But those soldiers, Tempe!" her mother said.

"I'll be fine, Mother. Remember, Flier is the fastest horse around here," Tempe answered quickly.

Now Tempe was a tall, strong girl. She could ride a horse faster than most people. When there was a tree to climb or a river to cross, Tempe was the first one who could do it. Yet now she felt a little afraid knowing she had to get past those soldiers who would want to take Flier. But she knew she had to go.

Tempe got Flier out of the barn and started off. As she rode past the soldiers, she saw them looking at her horse. One of them even tried to grab Flier, but she didn't stop.

When she got to the doctor, he gave her a little jar of dried rose hip tea. "Make some tea for your mother with this," he said. "I'll try to come to see her in a day or two, if I can get past the soldiers."

As she started back, Tempe was a little afraid because she knew the soldiers would be waiting to grab Flier. She was right. Three of them were standing in the road. "Stop, girl!" one shouted. "Let's see that horse!"

Then all the men were shouting at once. "Stop! Get off that horse!"

Tempe was really scared now, but she knew what she had to do. She slowed down almost to a stop. The men waited, thinking they had scared her into giving up her horse. But Tempe dug her feet into Flier's sides and shouted, "NOW, Flier! RUN!" Tempe and Flier crashed past the surprised soldiers and flew down the road.

Her thoughts were racing. She knew the men would come after Flier. Where could she hide him? He would not be safe in the barn. That's where they would look for him first. Could she tie him to a tree in the woods? No, they would look for him there, too.

Then Tempe had an idea. She raced up to the back door of the house and led Flier right into her own room!

She tied Flier to her bed and covered the windows. Then she thought, "They will hear him!" Quickly she got some rags and tied them around Flier's feet. She gave him a pat. "Shhhhhhh," she said. Tempe closed the door.

While giving her mother the rose hip tea,
Tempe told her what happened. Her mother was
very happy that Tempe was safe and very proud
of what she had done. "Tempe, what a smart
idea!" she said. "Who would think to look
for Flier in the house?"

Just then they heard a shout in the yard. Tempe
peeked out the window. Some soldiers ran into
the barn and came right out again. Then they
headed for the woods. "They won't find him
there!" Tempe smiled to herself.

Tempe slipped out after dark to get the horse some food and water from the barn, and she cleaned up after him. She had done this for three days when she looked out and saw that there was no more smoke from the fires in the air. The soldiers were gone! Tempe ran to tell her mother and then took Flier back to the barn.

That afternoon the doctor came. He was pleased to find Mrs. Wick feeling better. She told him what Tempe had done and how she had tricked the soldiers.

The doctor laughed. "Tempe, I can't wait to tell everyone!" he said.

Tempe just smiled.

The Six Wise Travelers

by Sally Jarvis

TRAVELER 1   Oh, look, friends. We have come to a
river. How will we get across?

TRAVELER 2   I see a boy with a boat. We will ask
him to take us.

TRAVELER 3   Boy! Boy! Will you take us across
the river in your boat?

BOY   There are too many of you for my
little boat.

TRAVELER 4   Silly boy! We are wiser than you. Let
us use your boat.

BOY   Very well. But I will not go with you.

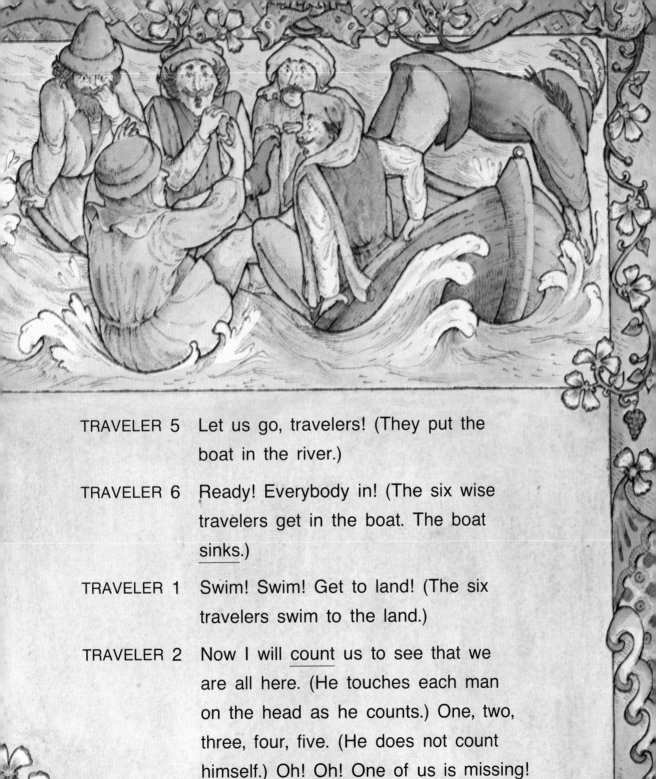

TRAVELER 5   Let us go, travelers! (They put the boat in the river.)

TRAVELER 6   Ready! Everybody in! (The six wise travelers get in the boat. The boat sinks.)

TRAVELER 1   Swim! Swim! Get to land! (The six travelers swim to the land.)

TRAVELER 2   Now I will count us to see that we are all here. (He touches each man on the head as he counts.) One, two, three, four, five. (He does not count himself.) Oh! Oh! One of us is missing!

TRAVELER 3 Silly! You are counting wrong! Let me do it. (He touches each man on the hand as he counts. He counts two hands for each man.) One, two, three, four, five, six, seven, eight, nine, ten. Why, there are ten of us! That is why the boat <u>sank</u>!

TRAVELER 4 Oh, you silly man. You counted two hands for each man! Let me do it. (He touches each man on the back as he counts.) One, two, three, four, five. (He does not count himself.) You are right! One traveler is missing! We will have to find him.

TRAVELER 5   (He sees the boy.) Boy! Go and find the missing traveler!

TRAVELER 6   We will give you a bag of <u>gold</u> if you find him.

BOY   Very well. Let me count you all first. One, two, three, four, five, six. (Of course he counts them all.) You are all here. I have found the missing man!

ALL SIX TRAVELERS

What a good boy! Here is your gold. When you grow up, maybe you will be as wise as we are! (The six wise travelers jump in the river and swim to the other side.)

Alphabetical Order

As you know, all the words in a glossary are listed in ABC order. This ABC order is called alphabetical order.

Here are some words. Write them in alphabetical order on your own paper.

maybe	thought	zoo	father
people	afternoon	bridge	cold

That was easy because all the words begin with different letters. But what happens when you have words that all start with the same letter? Those words are put into alphabetical order by the letters that come after the first letter.

Look at the words in the following list that begin with the letter **a**. They are in alphabetical order by their <u>second</u> letters as the lines show you. On your paper write the words that begin with **b** in alphabetical order.

a	b	out	begin
a	c	ross	ball
a	f	raid	blanket
a	n	ywhere	big

Words that have the same first and second letters must be put in alphabetical order by their third letters. List these words in alphabetical order on your paper.

angry	answer	another
anywhere	animal	and

Walk Home Tired, Billy Jenkins

by Ianthe Thomas

"Come on, Billy Jenkins, we've got a long way to walk to get home."

"I'm tired, Nina. I'm too tired to walk."

"Well . . . do you want to ride in my silver sailboat, Billy Jenkins? I'll tame that river for once and all times. So come on and sail with me.

"My sailboat's a silver, big one. It will sail us to Connecticut and back. You coming with me? Huh, Billy Jenkins, you want a ride?

"Or if the sea makes you swirly, boy, I'll take you on my smooth-riding plane. Just the two of us now, Billy Jenkins. Just the two of us for this plane ride.

"Yes. I can handle it gentle, too. Won't get sick on this ride. I'll take you so low we'll touch fence ivy and then back up again. Straight up, but not too fast. You won't get sick on this ride.

"So you coming with me, Billy Jenkins? You coming? Or do you want a country ride? I'll take you far out with me. Far out where the birds stick to the trees and then fly away together.

"Don't worry, we won't scare the birds when we go by. We'll glide, Billy Jenkins. We'll just glide.

"Maybe you don't like a riding plane. Maybe it's too tall and high. But I'd handle it <u>quiet</u> and gentle, and when it got too scary, <u>we'd</u> just glide. We don't have to take a plane, you know, Billy Jenkins. I got me a train as black as midnight <u>coal</u>. We'll shine it up proud, and it will take us fast and far—not too fast, just slow enough for us to see where the chipmunks hide.

"And when we come to where the tracks make a point we'll get off, Billy Jenkins. And you can put on the trainman's hat when I teach you my freedom dance. It's a spinning dance, but I'll hold you when we get dizzy. So come on, Billy Jenkins. Come on."

"Ah, you're just pretending, Nina. Just making believe."

"Well, then, walk home tired, Billy Jenkins. You just walk home tired if you won't ride with me."

"We really going far out, Nina? We really going to travel the world to the far and wide?"

"Yup, Billy Jenkins. To the far and wide. And when we're both too tired, we'll just glide."

"Here I come, Nina. Nina, wait for me!"

When I Went to Get a Drink

by John Ciardi

I said to a bug in the sink,
"Are you taking a swim or a drink?"
  "I," said the bug,
  "Am a sea-going tug.
Am I headed for land, do you think?"

"What a silly!" I said. "That's no sea—
It's a sink!"—"A sink it may be.
  But I'd sooner I think
  Be at sea in the sink
Than sink in the sea, sir," said he.

The Rabbit and the Turnip

a Chinese fable by Richard Sadler

One winter day, when snow lay deep on the ground, Little Rabbit went out to look for food, and he found two turnips. He gobbled up one of them. Then he said, "It is snowing so hard and it is so very cold that maybe Little Donkey has nothing to eat. I will take him my other turnip."

Off he ran to Little Donkey's house. But Little Donkey was out, so Little Rabbit left the turnip on Little Donkey's doorstep and hopped back home.

Now Little Donkey had also gone out to look for food, and he found some potatoes. When he got home and saw the turnip, he was very surprised. Who could have put it there? Then he said to himself, "It is snowing so hard, and it is so very cold. Maybe Little Sheep has nothing to eat. I will take it to her."

At once he rolled the turnip to Little Sheep's house. But there was no sign of Little Sheep, so he left the turnip on Little Sheep's table and trotted back home.

At the same time, Little Sheep, who had also been looking for food, had found a cabbage and was happily trotting home to eat it.

When she got to her house and found the turnip, she was surprised. Who could have put it there? Little Sheep decided to give the turnip to Little Doe. It was snowing so hard and it was so very cold she knew Little Doe would need something to eat.

So Little Sheep took the turnip to Little Doe's house. But there was no one at home, so she left the turnip on Little Doe's window sill, and off she went.

It so happened that Little Doe was also out looking for food, and she found some fresh green leaves. She, too, was very surprised to find the turnip waiting for her at home. "I will give this beautiful turnip to Little Rabbit," she said to herself. "It is snowing so hard and it is so very cold that maybe he has nothing to eat."

At once Little Doe ran to Little Rabbit's house. And there was Little Rabbit, fast asleep. Little Doe did not want to wake him up, so she put the turnip quietly inside the doorway and hurried away.

When Little Rabbit woke up and found the turnip, he thought he must be dreaming. He rubbed his eyes. Then he said to himself, "How kind of someone to give me this turnip!" And he gobbled it all up.

Nuts and Ideas

When you crack open a nutshell, what do you find inside? Yes, the nut, crisp and good. The shell is an important part of the nut, but what's inside the shell is what we really want. In much the same way we want to get all we can out of what we read. We want to find the most important thought, or the <u>main</u> idea, of what we read.

Sometimes it's easy to spot the main idea, but other times it's hard. See if you can find the main idea in the following stories.

One part of our country is <u>prairie</u>. It is flat, rolling land that doesn't have many trees. Winter on the prairie can be very cold, and summer can be very hot. But the prairie is a good place for plants to grow. Most of the corn we eat is grown on the prairie in the summer.

Which of the following names gives the main idea of this story?

Growing Corn
The Prairie
Summer and Winter

What a mess! Used pots, pans, and bowls were everywhere in the kitchen. There was something white all over the table, and something sticky and yellow was all over the floor. But now the cake was done, and Carla and Jim felt proud and happy. What a wonderful birthday surprise for their mother!

What would be the best name for this story?

Something Sticky
Kitchen Magic
Mother's Birthday Surprise

Little Green Riding Hood

by Gianni Rodari

 Once upon a time there was a little girl called Little Yellow Riding Hood.

 No! RED Riding Hood!

 Oh yes, of course, Red Riding Hood. Well, one day her mother called and said, "Little Green Riding Hood—"

 Red!

42

 <u>Sorry!</u> Red. "Now, Red Riding Hood, go to Aunt Kitty and take her these potatoes."

 No! It doesn't go like that! "Go to Grandma and take her these cakes."

 All right. So the little girl went off, and in the woods she met a bear.

 What a mess you're making of it! It was a <u>wolf!</u>

 And the wolf said, "What's six times eight?"

 No! No! The wolf asked her where she was going.

So he did. And Little Black Riding Hood answered—

 Red! Red!! Red!!!

 She answered, "I'm going to the store to buy some tomatoes."

 No, she didn't. She said, "I'm going to my grandma, who is sick, but I've lost my way."

 Of course! And the horse said—

 What horse? It was a wolf.

44

So it was. And this is what it said. "Take the 75 bus, get out at Main Street, turn right, and at the first doorway you'll find three steps. Leave the steps where they are, but pick up the dime you'll find on them, and buy yourself a pack of gum."

 Grandpa, you're very bad at telling stories. You get them all wrong. But all the same, I would like some gum.

 All right. Here is your dime.

And the old man turned back to his newspaper.

Jo, Flo, and Yolanda

by Carol de Poix

Jo, Flo, and Yolanda are sisters. They look like each other.

They have the same birthday and are the same age.

They go to the same school and have the same teacher, who teaches them the same things.

They live on the same block in the same building in the very same apartment.

They have the same mother, who kisses them good-by every morning before she takes the subway to work.

And they have the same father, who leaves for work after dinner at night and comes home in the morning and starts breakfast while everyone is still sound asleep.

And they have the same big brother, George, who walks with them to school in the morning on his way to high school. And he fixes dinner at night while they help him and set the table so it's all ready when their mother comes home from work.

But Jo, Flo, and Yolanda are also very different.
In fact it's quite easy to tell them apart. Jo is just
a little taller. Flo is just a little thinner. And Yolanda
is just a little fatter.

Jo likes to read books about people in faraway
places and look at the pictures. And she likes to
think of stories all her own.

Flo likes to jump and run in the park. She can run
faster than anyone on the block and can throw a
baseball better than anyone, except a girl who
lives in the apartment down the hall and a boy her
age who lives in the building across the street.

What Yolanda likes to do is help George make things in the kitchen. She likes to make arroz con pollo most of all. That's rice with chicken. Even more, she likes to eat the things she makes.

And when she grows up, Jo wants to go to see all those places in the books and write more books for other people to read.

Flo wants to be a shortstop on a baseball team. First base would be OK, but shortstop is what she really wants the most.

Yolanda wants to have her own restaurant, like the Rodriguez restaurant on the corner. Then she and George can cook all day, and everyone from all over the city can come in and eat.

So even though Jo, Flo, and Yolanda all climb into the same bed at night, under the same big blue blanket, and hear the same bedtime story from their mother, and even though when the lights are out, they see the same street light shining in their window, what's inside their heads is not the same at all.

Each one has her very own dream that makes her special and different from anyone else in the world.

At the <u>edge</u> of the world
It is growing light.
The trees stand shining.
I like it.
It is growing light.

<u>PAPAGO</u>

As my eyes
Search the prairie,
I feel the summer in the spring.

CHIPPEWA

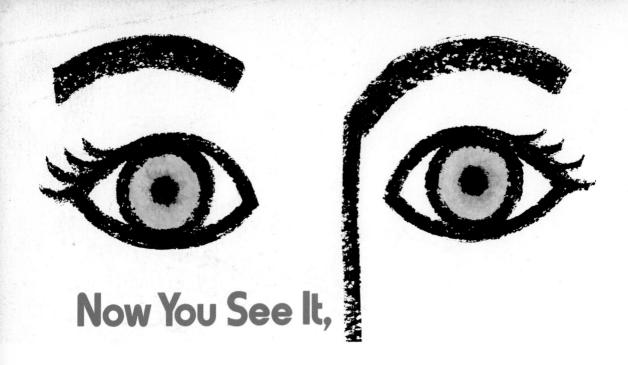

Now You See It,

You just <u>blinked</u>. Your eyelids just went down and up. There you go again. Down and up. And in a few seconds more, down and up again.

A blink lasts less than half a second. Your eyes really do close. But it happens so fast you don't really miss anything.

Blinks come every two to ten seconds. If you had to think about blinking, you'd be too busy to do anything else. All day you'd just sit around counting. 1, 2, blink. 1, 2, blink.

Now You Don't

by Constance Whitman Baher

But blinking takes care of itself. You can try to stop. But you can't do it for more than a few seconds. See — there it goes. Blink!

Blinking is the way your eyelids keep house. It cleans away dust from your eyes.

Your eyelids get some help from your eyelashes. They help keep dust and dirt out of your eyes, too. But they're always falling out, right? Eyelashes last no longer than three to five months. But you do have 400 of them. So if one falls out next time you blink, don't worry. You still have 399 more.

Making Hard Sentences Easy

Have you at any time read a very long sentence and had trouble understanding it? Some long sentences are hard to understand because they have many little sentences in them. You need to find out what those little sentences are.

Here is a long sentence. Read it and think about what the little sentences in it are.

> After the wolf gobbled up the ducks, the people got together and decided to build a wall.

Did you find these little sentences in it?

> The wolf gobbled up the ducks.
> The people got together.
> The people decided to build a wall.

Now write the following sentence on your own paper and then write its little sentences.

> When we could not find the cat anywhere inside, we searched the yard and found it.

GRRR!

The Man Who Didn't Wash His Dishes

by Phyllis Krasilovsky

There once was a man who lived all alone in a
little house on the edge of a town. He always
cooked his own dinner, cleaned the house by
himself, and made his own bed.

One night he came home feeling very, very
hungry, so he made himself a big, big dinner.

It was a very good dinner—he liked to cook and could make good things to eat—but there was so much of it that he was very, very tired by the time he'd finished. He just sat back, as full as he could be, and decided he'd leave the dishes till the next night, and then he would wash them all at once.

BLAIR DRAWSON

But the next night he was <u>TWICE</u> as hungry, so he cooked TWICE as big a dinner and took TWICE as long to eat it and was TWICE as tired by the time he'd finished.

So he left THOSE dishes in the sink, too.

Well, as the days went by, he got hungrier and hungrier and more and more tired, and so he never washed his dishes. After a while there were so MANY dirty dishes that they didn't all fit in the sink. So he started to pile them on the table.

Soon the table was so full that he started to put them on his bookshelves.

And when THEY were full, he put them just everywhere he could find a place.

Soon he had them all piled on the floor, too. In fact the floor got to be so FULL of dishes that he had a hard time getting into his house at night. THEY WERE EVEN PILED AGAINST THE DOOR!

Then one night he looked in his closet and found that there WASN'T ONE CLEAN DISH LEFT! He was hungry enough to eat out of anything, so he ate out of the soap dish from the bathroom. It was too dirty for him to use again the NEXT night, so he used one of his ash trays.

Soon he had used up all his ash trays. THEN he ate out of some clean flowerpots he found. When THEY were all used up, he ate out of his candy dishes and drank water from vases.

He used up EVERYTHING, even the pots he cooked his food in, and he didn't know what to do! He was SO unhappy. His whole house was full of dirty dishes and dirty flowerpots and dirty ash trays and dirty candy dishes and dirty pots and a dirty soap dish. He couldn't even find his books or his clock or even his BED any more! He couldn't sit down to think because even his chairs were filled with dishes, and he couldn't find the sink so he could wash them!

But THEN IT STARTED TO RAIN!

And the man got an idea.

He drove his big truck around to the side of the house and piled all the dishes and all the vases and all the flowerpots and all the ash trays and all the candy dishes and the soap dish on it and drove the truck out into the rain.

The rain fell on everything, and soon the dishes were clean again. THE RAIN HAD WASHED THEM!

Then the man carried everything back into the house again. He put the dishes in the dish closet, the pots in the pot closet, the ash trays on the tables, the candy dishes on the shelves, the flowerpots back where he found them, the vases where the vases go, and the soap dish in the bathroom. He was so very, very tired after carrying everything back and putting it away that he decided that from then on he would always wash his dishes just as soon as he had finished his dinner.

The next night when he came home, he cooked his dinner, and when he had finished eating it, he washed the dishes and put them right away. He did this every night after that, too.

He is very happy now. He can find his chairs, and he can find his clock, and he can find his BED. It is easy for him to get into his house, too, because there are no more dishes piled on the floor—or anywhere!

Collection 2

ī	ů		ü	nd	ng	nt
might	stood		threw	mind	rang	bent
tight	foot		goof	sand	bring	cent
	roof	or	roof	pound	bang	
				spend	song	

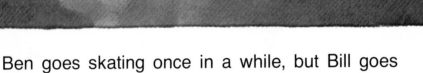

1. Ben goes skating once in a while, but Bill goes often.

2. A nickel is the same as five pennies.

3. The book was so big and heavy I could hardly pick it up.

4. Some chicks hatched, but some did not come out of the egg.

5. An apple a day keeps the doctor away.

Words You Can Read

cen ter	sup pose	ac cent
Cin dy	mat ter	Pen ny
Nan cy	sog gy	rub ber
un less	dad dy	les son
num ber	writ ten	Fan ny

accountant	goof	prickly
agree	gravity	puzzle
allowance	Indian Ocean	rhythm
amusement	Jupiter	sailor
areaway	Mars	scramble
bumble	meadow	sewer
cereal	medicine	steering
comfort	mystery	suit
computer	nurse	symbol
couple	office	thread
daisy	operate	tomorrow
empty	pajamas	universe
figure	patient	vacation
finally	paw	veterinarian
germs	planet	wart hog

Big Sister

and Little Sister by Charlotte Zolotow

Once there was a big sister and a little sister.
The big sister always took care. Even when she
was jumping rope, she took care that her little
sister stayed on the sidewalk.

When she rode her bike, she gave her little
sister a ride. When she was walking to school,
she took little sister's hand and helped her
across the street. When they were playing in the
fields, she made sure little sister didn't get lost.

When they were sewing, she made sure little
sister's needle was <u>threaded</u> and that little sister
held the scissors the right way.

Big sister took care of everything, and little
sister thought there was nothing big sister
couldn't do.

Little sister would sometimes cry, but big sister
always made her stop. First she'd put her arm
around her. Then she'd hold out her
handkerchief and say, "Here, blow."

Big sister knew everything.

"Don't do it like that," she'd say. "Do it this way."

And little sister did. Nothing could bother big sister. She knew too much.

But one day little sister wanted to be alone. She was tired of big sister saying,
"Sit here.
Go there.
Do it this way.
Come along."

And while big sister was getting lemonade and cookies for them, little sister slipped away — out of the house, out of the yard, down the road, and into the meadow, where daisies and grass hid her. Pretty soon she heard big sister calling, calling, and calling. But she didn't answer.

She heard big sister's voice getting louder when she was close and fainter when she went the other way, calling, calling.

Little sister leaned back in the daisies. She thought about lemonade and cookies. She thought about the book big sister had promised to read to her.

She thought about
big sister saying,
"Sit here.
Go there.
Do it this way.
Come along."

No one told little sister anything now. The daisies <u>bent</u> in the sun. A big bee <u>bumbled</u> by.

The weeds felt <u>prickly</u> under her legs. But she didn't move. She heard big sister's voice coming back. It came closer and closer. And suddenly big sister was so near little sister could have touched her.

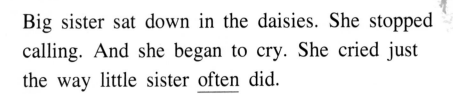

Big sister sat down in the daisies. She stopped calling. And she began to cry. She cried just the way little sister <u>often</u> did.

When the little sister cried, the big one comforted her. But there was no one to put an arm around big sister. No one took out a handkerchief and said, "Here, blow." Big sister just sat there crying, alone.

Little sister stood up, but big sister didn't even see her because she was crying so completely.

Little sister went over and put her arm around big sister. She took out her handkerchief and said kindly, "Here, blow."

Big sister did. Then the little sister hugged her.

"Where have you been?" big sister asked.

"Never <u>mind</u>," said the little sister. "Let's go home and have some lemonade."

And from that day on little sister and big sister both took care of each other because little sister had learned from big sister, and now they both knew how.

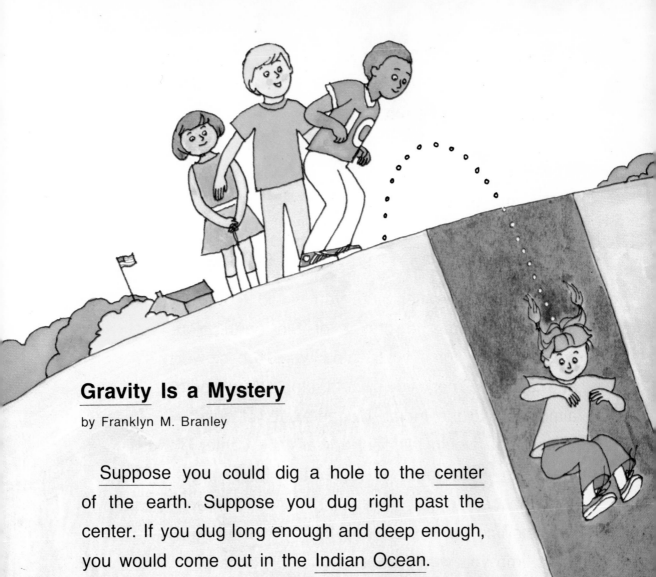

Gravity Is a Mystery

by Franklyn M. Branley

Suppose you could dig a hole to the center of the earth. Suppose you dug right past the center. If you dug long enough and deep enough, you would come out in the Indian Ocean.

If you jumped into the hole, you would fall down. Down and down you would go.

You would fall faster and faster toward the center of the earth. When you reached the center, you would be going so fast you could not stop. You would go right past the center.

75

Then, on the other side, you would move up and away from the center of the earth. You would fall up for a while. You would go slower and slower. Then you would stop. You would almost get to the Indian Ocean—but not quite.

Now you would fall back toward the center of the earth. You would go faster and faster, right past the center. But you would not quite reach your starting point. Back and forth you would go. Each time you would go a shorter distance past the center.

Gravity would make you fall toward the center of the earth. When you moved past the center, gravity would pull you back again. After a long, long time you would stop moving. You would stay at the center of the earth.

Gravity pulls things toward the center of the earth. When you run downhill, or uphill, gravity pulls you. When you throw a ball up, gravity pulls it down. When you sit, gravity holds you down. When you lie down, gravity holds you to the bed. But what is gravity?

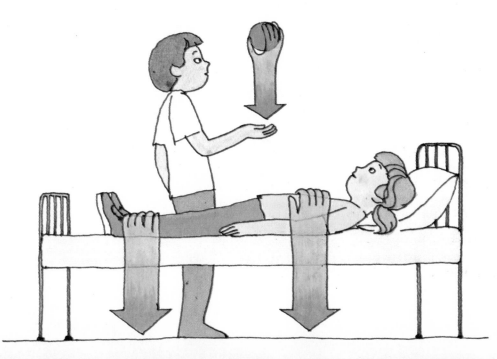

We know gravity is everywhere even though we can't see it. We know it pulls on every rock and every grain of sand. It pulls on everything.

The gravity of the earth pulls things toward the center of the earth. You know this when you try to lift a heavy stone. Gravity pulls it down. The more the stone weighs, the more gravity pulls on it. To lift the stone, you must pull up harder than gravity pulls down.

Lift a baby. Then try to lift a grown-up. The more they weigh, the harder it is to lift them.

You know how much gravity pulls on you. Do you weigh 60 pounds? That means the pull of the earth's gravity on you is 60 pounds. How much you weigh tells how much gravity pulls on you. How much a stone weighs tells you how much gravity pulls on the stone.

The earth has gravity, and so does the moon. The earth's gravity pulls you toward the center of the earth. If you were on the moon, the moon's gravity would pull you toward the center of the moon. The moon has less gravity than the earth has. This means the moon's gravity does not pull as hard as the earth's gravity.

Do you weigh 60 pounds? If you were on the moon, you would weigh only 10 pounds. The pull of the moon's gravity on you would be only 10 pounds.

Gravity is everywhere—on the earth, on the moon, on Jupiter, on Mars, and on all the other planets. All things in the universe have gravity. The sun has gravity, and so does every other star.

The gravity of the earth holds things on the earth. It holds down rugs and tables and you and me. Gravity makes a ball come down. It makes us work hard to lift a heavy stone.

We know where gravity is; it is everywhere. And we know what gravity does. But no one knows exactly what gravity is. Gravity is a mystery.

Have you ever missed the end of a good TV show? Or did you ever have to stop reading an exciting story right in the middle of it? When that happened, did you try to decide how the show or story might have ended?

Read the following story beginnings and make up your own ending for each one. Then talk about your ideas for endings with some friends and your teacher.

The Oak Street Mystery

It was almost dark when Cindy, Jim, and Don walked home from school after the basketball game. There were no cars on the street. Only a big mover's truck was going by slowly.

"Come on!" said Jim. He didn't say how scary the dark empty house they were in front of was, but all of them were thinking about it.

"Look!" yelled Don suddenly. "Someone is in there!" In one window of the old empty house a light was going on and off.

"Let's get out of here!" yelled Jim.

"No! Come on!" said Don. "This is a real mystery! Let's see what it's all about!"

"OK!" said Cindy. "Come on, Jim!"

The Missing Money

Tom walked into the store with a happy look on his face. He had enough money in his pocket to buy something really nice for his sister's birthday. He had stopped near home to buy some ice cream, but he had a lot of money left over.

Then he had walked the four blocks to the store. Now that he was there, he looked around. Then he saw it—a beautiful popcorn popper. He knew Nancy would like it. Tom looked to see how much it was. He had just enough money! "I'll take that," he said to Mr. Sparks as he reached into his pocket. The pocket was empty!

I Should Have
Stayed
in Bed!

by Joan M. Lexau

Some days it doesn't pay to get up. Some days
you can't do anything right. One day I woke up.
The sun was shining. Birds were singing.

I got dressed. I put on my shoes. I tied my
shoelaces. The shoes were on the wrong feet.
When I untied the shoelaces, I made two knots.
So I left the shoes on the wrong feet. I went
down to breakfast.

"Good morning, dear," said my mother. "Why are you wearing your Cub Scout suit? Tomorrow is Cub Scout day."

"Good morning, Sam," said my father. "Your shoes are on the wrong feet. What's the matter with you today? This isn't like you."

I got dressed all over again. When I tried to untie the shoelaces, they broke. I put the shoes on the right feet. I went down again to breakfast.

"Not so much sugar on your cereal, dear," my mother said.

"I like it this way," I said. I put some more sugar on my cereal. At the bottom it was all soggy sugar. I ate it all up. It was terrible.

I went to call for Albert. Good old Albert. My best friend. "Albert. Hey, Albert," I yelled at his window.

"Albert left. It's late," his mother said. That Albert. Some friend!

I took off for school. I saw a nickel in the street. "Good," I said. "Something good at last."

I went over to pick it up. My foot kicked it into a sewer. "Boy, I should have stayed in bed," I said.

I got to school when the first bell rang.

"Here comes Sam the snail," Albert said. "What took you so long?"

I threw a notebook at him. He ducked. The notebook hit Amy Lou.

"You could have killed me," Amy Lou said.
"I'm going to tell." She ran into the school.

I ran after her. "Amy Lou," I said. "Amy Lou,
Amy Lou, Amy Lou."

Amy Lou went into our room. "Sam tried to kill
me!" she yelled.

The teacher wasn't there. So everybody ran
around the room.

"Watch me," I said. "Watch how fast I can go."
I turned around and around and around, faster
and faster.

The second bell rang. Everybody sat down.
Everybody but me. I fell down. The teacher came
in.

"Well, Sam?" said the teacher.

"I got dizzy," I said.

"Oh. Go see the nurse," said the teacher. So I did.

Boy, was the nurse mad when she found out why I got dizzy. She told me off. She gave me a note for my teacher. The teacher told me off, too. She told me to open my reader and read.

I read, "Bob walked down the dark street. He was getting colder and colder. By and by he was a snowman."

Everybody laughed.

"He saw a snowman," said the teacher. "Maybe you are still dizzy, Sam. Amy Lou, it is your turn."

Amy Lou read it right. She always does. Albert gave me a note. I opened it up. The teacher saw it. "Read the note out loud," she said.

What could I do? I read it out loud. It said, "Can you read this fast? Eye yam. Eye yam. Eye ree lee yam. Eye man ut."

Everybody laughed. I didn't look at Albert.

"You read that very well," said the teacher. "But after this when you and Albert have something to say, say it to all of us. No more notes."

I thought lunchtime would never come. But at last it did. I didn't wait for Albert.

"Sam, Albert is calling you," Amy Lou said.

"Albert?" I said. "Who is Albert? I don't know any Albert."

I ran all the way home. I said over and over,
"I should have stayed in bed. I should have
stayed in bed."

When I got home, I said, "Why not? It can only help. Things can't get any worse." So I went to my room. I put on my pajamas. I went to bed and counted to one hundred.

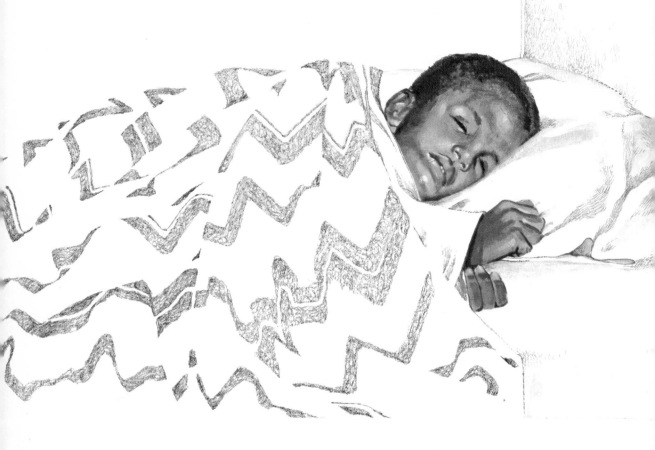

"I'll call the doctor," my mother said. "Now I know something is the matter."

"I'm all right," I said. "I'm starting the day over."

"Oh," said my mother. She looked at me as if I were crazy. But she didn't call the doctor.

I got up and put on my robe and slippers. I asked for some cereal. I put just a little sugar on it.

Then I got dressed and ran to school. I didn't see Albert. I heard the first bell ring. I heard the second bell ring. Everybody was in school. No, not everybody. There was Albert by the door. "You're late," he said.

"Well, so are you," I said.

"I know," Albert said. "I saw you coming, so I waited for you. We can both stay after school."

Good old Albert. Good old best friend Albert. We went into our room.

"Sam and Albert are late," Amy Lou said.

"So I see," said the teacher.

"They'll have to stay after school, won't they?"
said Amy Lou.

"Yes, they will," said the teacher.

"You know what?" said Amy Lou. "You know
what? Sam has his slippers on!"

Everybody laughed. What a crazy day!

"Amy Lou," said the teacher, "you will have to
stay after school. You talk too much."

I looked at Albert. Albert looked at me. It didn't
look like such a bad day after all.

the drum

by Nikki Giovanni

daddy says the world is
a drum tight and hard
and i told him
i'm gonna beat
out my own rhythm

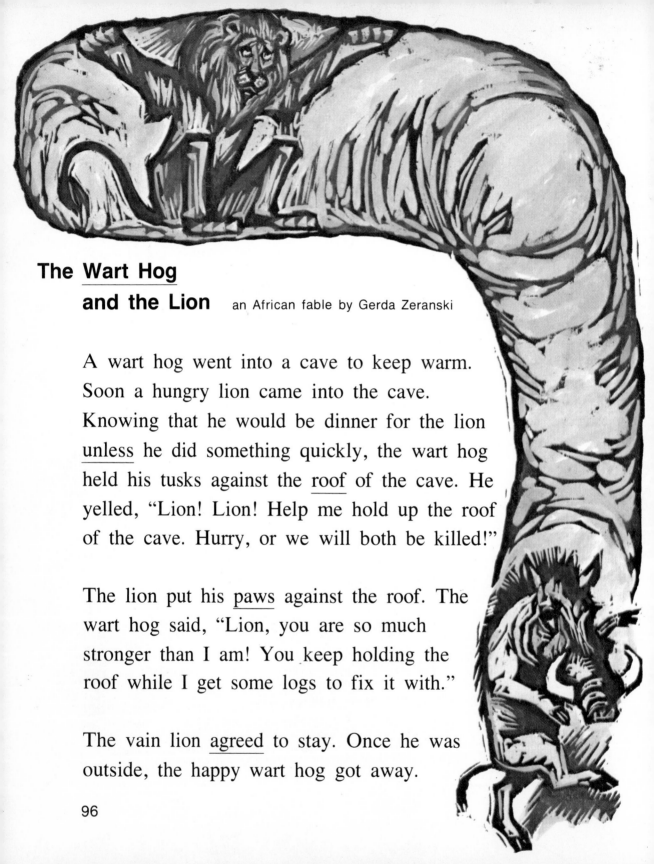

The Wart Hog
and the Lion   an African fable by Gerda Zeranski

A wart hog went into a cave to keep warm.
Soon a hungry lion came into the cave.
Knowing that he would be dinner for the lion
unless he did something quickly, the wart hog
held his tusks against the roof of the cave. He
yelled, "Lion! Lion! Help me hold up the roof
of the cave. Hurry, or we will both be killed!"

The lion put his paws against the roof. The
wart hog said, "Lion, you are so much
stronger than I am! You keep holding the
roof while I get some logs to fix it with."

The vain lion agreed to stay. Once he was
outside, the happy wart hog got away.

ə kōd fər ū

Patient?

How do you say the word **patient**? If you don't
know, you know where to find out, don't you? If
you look up **patient** in the Glossary at the end of
this book, you'll find this.

pā′shənt

Does that look like it's <u>written</u> in a code? It is. It is
in a code that tells you what the sounds in the
word are. And the key to the code is on page 310.
Turn to page 310 and look at this code. Next, look
at the shorter key at the bottom of this page. You
will see that the <u>symbols</u> that may <u>puzzle</u> you are
given in both keys.

a apple, ā able, ã air, ä arm; e elevator, ē each, ėr earth; i itch, ī ivy;
o October, ō open, ô all, ôr order; oi oil, ou out; u up, ů put, ü glue,
ū use; th thin, ᴛʜ then, zh measure; ə about, occur, until

Now try to use this key to <u>figure</u> out how to say
pa tient (pā'shənt). Once you have figured out
what sounds the symbols stand for, you have to
know which part of the word is <u>accented</u>. Look at
(pā'shənt) again. Something tells you which part of
the word is accented. What is it? Now say **patient**.

Using this key is not hard when you get used to it.
And now is a good time to start. Here are two
riddles written in the same symbols. Use the key
to read each one. Answers are upside down.

hwuts blak ənd
hwīt ənd
red ôl ō'vər

hwī did ŦHə
chik'ən kros
ŦHə rōd

ə nūz'pā'pər

far sum foul pər'pas

98

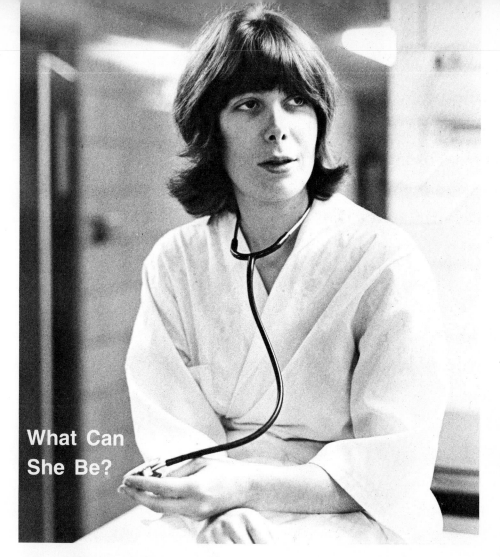

What Can She Be?

A Veterinarian

by Gloria and Esther Goldreich

This is Dr. Penny. She is a veterinarian, an animal doctor. Her patients are mostly cats, dogs, birds, and rabbits. But she knows how to take care of cows and horses, pigs and sheep, and even lions, tigers, and other animals that you see in the zoo and circus.

Dr. Penny works at an animal hospital. First she and another doctor check the sick animals in the hospital. After the doctors have checked all the patients, they examine the animals that have just come in and decide how to help them.

Rex's owner brought him to see Dr. Penny because he was limping. Dr. Penny will examine him and find out why he is dragging his leg.

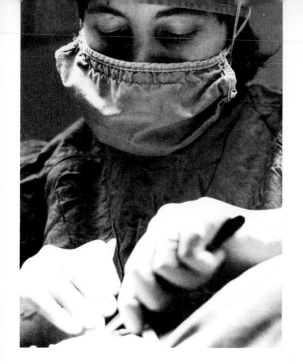
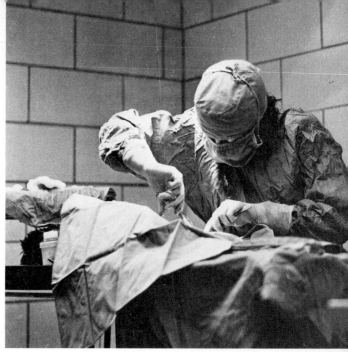

Dr. Penny decides to take an X-ray picture of the inside of Rex's leg. After she looks at the X-ray picture, she knows just what is wrong with Rex. His leg is broken. Dr. Penny will <u>operate</u> on his leg.

Dr. Penny gets ready for the operation by washing her hands carefully with hot water and a strong soap. This is to make sure that no <u>germs</u> get on the dog. She also wears a clean mask, cap, and gown and <u>rubber</u> gloves. The operation does not hurt Rex because Dr. Penny gives him some <u>medicine</u> that puts him to sleep for a while.

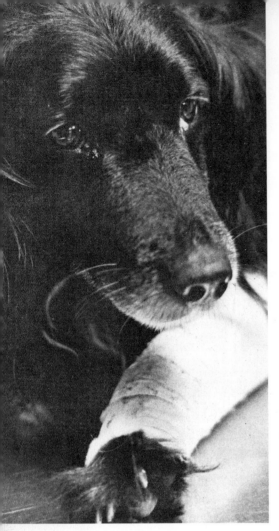

During the operation Dr. Penny puts in a special pin to hold the broken bone together. She also puts a cast on to hold Rex's leg straight until it heals. Rex has some pain after the operation, but soon he will be ready to go home and run around and have fun.

Afternoons at the veterinarian's office are very busy for Dr. Penny because that is when most people bring their animals in to see her.

Dr. Penny gives some animals shots so they don't get sick. These shots are like the ones doctors give children so they will not get some illnesses.

It is also a part of a veterinarian's job to keep animals' teeth clean. A look into an animal's mouth tells Dr. Penny if it has healthy gums and strong teeth. Cats and dogs must have their eyes and ears checked, too.

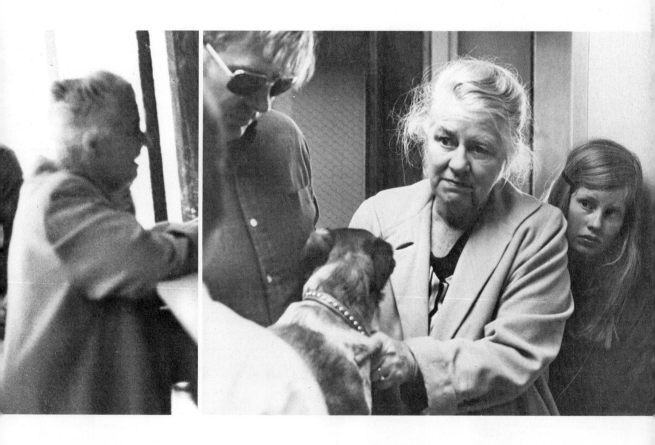

Sometimes there is a lot of excitement in an animal hospital. A dog was just hit by a car. His family rushed him to Dr. Penny's hospital.

Katie and Peter are very worried about their pet. They have taken care of him since he was a little pup, and they are worried about what will happen to him. Their grandmother is worried, too. She holds the leash while Dr. Penny examines the dog. All is well. The dog is a little scared, but he is not hurt. He has learned a good <u>lesson</u>. Next time he won't chase cars!

"You must not let your dog run out in the street," Dr. Penny tells the children. They say they will be more careful, and the dog goes home with his happy family.

All afternoon Dr. Penny's phone rings. Owners call to ask about pets that are staying in the hospital. Children call to ask questions about what to feed their pets.

At the end of the day Dr. Penny is tired. She has worked very hard and helped lots of animals. But when she gets home, she is still ready to play with her own dogs.

Dr. Penny loves her work. She thinks being a veterinarian is exciting and the very best kind of work for her to do.

Mushy Eggs

by Florence Adams

My name is David, and I am eight years old. This
is a picture of me and my brother, Sam. Sam
has red hair, and he is only four. We live in a
brownstone house in Brooklyn with our mom. It's
the one with the red flowers in the window box.

Our mom works in the city on a computer. One
time we got to go to her office, and I made a
computer card with holes in it that said my name.

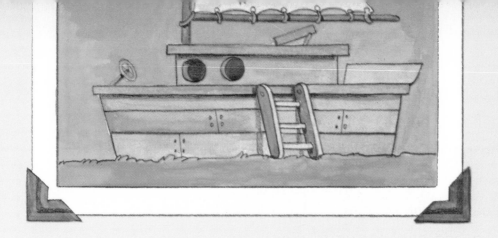

Mom is also a good builder. She builds closets and bookcases and things.

This is the ship that she made for us in the backyard. It has a sail and a hatch and a steering wheel. It even has a telephone to the lower deck made of tin cans.

This is our dad's house. He doesn't live with us. Our dad is an accountant, and that means he is very smart with numbers.

Dad comes to see Sam and me every week. Sometimes he takes us out to a special place or to the park to play baseball.

Sometimes we play at Dad's house. He has lots of toys and stuff for us to play with.

This is our baby sitter, Fanny. She loves us, too.

Fanny takes care of us while Mom is at work. She comes early every morning. The first thing she does is change into her blue dress that she keeps in our closet. It's a nice dress.

Then she makes our breakfast. "Well, what do you want me to make today?" she says.

"MUSHY EGGS," we yell.

"Mushy eggs, always mushy eggs," she says. "OK, OK. Mushy eggs."

Mushy eggs are like <u>scrambled</u> eggs, only mushier. Fanny makes the best mushy eggs in the world.

After breakfast Jimmy, the vegetable man, parks in front of our house. We all go out, and Fanny shops for dinner. Sometimes Jimmy gives me an old <u>apple</u> to give his horse.

Once Fanny got a bag of lemons from Jimmy and made lemonade. Then she found an old box and helped us make a lemonade stand. It was fun selling lemonade, except Sam kept testing it, so we made only 12 cents.

In the afternoon Fanny sends us to do the jobs we do for our allowance. My job is to take out the trash. I get 25 cents. Sam wanted an outside job, too, so Mom said he could sweep the areaway. He only gets 7 cents.

There are lots of ways to spend an allowance, so it doesn't last very long. In the summer Ralph, the ice cream man, comes everyday. "Too many times," says Fanny. I like a vanilla cone. It costs 12 cents. Sam likes an empty cone. That costs only 2 cents.

Sometimes the Moon Ride stops near our house. It's a ride like in the amusement park, only it's on a big truck. It goes back and forth. I like to sit way up high, but Fanny makes the man put Sam down near the bottom so he won't fall off.

On rainy days, when we have to stay inside, Fanny plays games with us. Sometimes we play horse, and Fanny lets us ride on her back. Sometimes we play opera. I play my guitar. Sam bangs on his drum. And Fanny sings songs. We laugh a lot.

Sometimes she tells us stories about when she was a little girl in another country far away. And about when she was eight years old and came to Brooklyn with her mom and dad.

That's how life was—games and lemonade and laughing with our Fanny—until a <u>couple</u> of weeks ago.

Then one afternoon Fanny told us she was going back to the country where she was born. "It's beautiful there," she said, "and I want to see all my old friends and cousins. I never told you this," she said, "but I cried hard when I left because I was so sad to leave all my friends."

Mommy took us to the boat on the day Fanny left. It was the biggest boat I ever saw. Fanny had her own room with a bed and a chair and a little sink. We got to go all over the boat. There were stores and a restaurant and a movie and a big swimming pool.

Then all of a sudden a funny thing happened. At first I didn't understand it. People were hugging and kissing each other, and a lot of people were crying. I looked up at Fanny, and I felt funny inside. Then I knew why everyone was crying. Someone they loved was going away.

One of the sailors came around and told us we
had to leave. Sam just stood there, hugging
Fanny's leg. Finally, Mommy picked him up. We all
gave Fanny a big hug and kisses, and we went off
the boat. We stood on the dock and waved to
Fanny and watched the boat sail away. Then we
went home.

I went to my room to be alone for a while. I felt
awful. I was thinking nothing would ever be good
any more. And I began to cry all over again. Mom
came in and held me tight. "Fanny is very special
to us," she said. And she cried, too.

But Sam wasn't crying. He was throwing toys all around. He was really mad. Mostly at Fanny, I think, because he kept saying, "I hate that Fanny what left us!"

Then he looked in the closet, and there was Fanny's blue dress. That's when Sam started to cry, too.

Mom stayed home with us the week after Fanny left, and we had fun—like when we're on vacation.

Now we have a new baby sitter, named Molly. She's nice, and she bakes good cookies. Maybe I'll love Molly, too, someday. But she doesn't know how to make mushy eggs.

We Could Be Friends

by Myra Cohn Livingston

We could be friends
Like friends are supposed to be.
You, picking up the telephone
Calling me

    to come over and play
    or take a walk,
    finding a place
    to sit and talk,

Or just <u>goof</u> around
Like friends do,
Me, picking up the telephone
Calling you.

116

Collection 3

Words You Can Read

bat tle   ad mire

cher ry   ex cuse

sad dle   thun der

pud dle   ad mit

mir ror   mis ter

mut ter   trum pet

peb ble   gar den

ô   ld

fought   wild

yawn   child

jaws   fold

bought

one wolf ⟶ two wolves

there is   here is   who is

there i s   here i s   who i s

there's   here's   who's

118

Words You Can Read

address	flute	realize
Afro	gallop	rein
agent	garage	reservation
alarming	giant	return
alike	glance	sheo
appear	gravel	shovel
balance	heart	shrill
bridle	helchetu aloh	shrub
buffalo	hey-a-hey	single
businesslike	homesteader	Sioux
castle	Indian	slain
celebrate	invisible	South Dakota
chahumpi ska	lumberjack	spread
charcoal	mayor	strange
container	message	tambourine
cord	molasses	tepee
difficult	official	terrarium
entrance	parade	usual
envelope	porch	Wasichus
favorite	post	windmill

Little Yellow Fur

by Wilma Pitchford Hays

"Play close to the house," her mother told
Susanna. "South Dakota is wild country. Not like
the town where we used to live."

Susanna had heard wolves howl in the night. But
Papa said wolves would not come to the house.

She and her mother and father were home-
steaders. They had come to live on free land near
the Rosebud Indian Reservation in 1913. Papa
liked it here. Susanna liked whatever Papa liked.
But Susanna's mother said to Papa, "I know the
Indians don't want us here on land that used to
be theirs."

Susanna thought the Indians might become good
friends anyway. They often rode by on their ponies.
They always waved to her. Often they stopped
and talked to Papa.

The Indians liked to look at Susanna and at her
big dog, Terk. They called him Dog-big-as-a-pony.
One day Terk let them come close to admire
Susanna. The Indian women touched Susanna's
blond curly hair. Little Yellow Fur, they named her.

They gave her chunks of brown sugar. "Chahumpi
ska," they said, which in Sioux means "juice-of-
the-tree."

Susanna ate it and wanted more. "Chahumpi ska?" she asked. The Indian women laughed when Susanna said the Sioux word. They clapped their hands. Little Yellow Fur learned fast! "Hey-a-hey!" they cried. "Hey-a-hey!" Susanna knew this meant "Wonderful. You're doing fine!" She laughed with the Indians and said, "Hey-a-hey!"

The next day Susanna saw Red Cloud on his spotted pony. He and Papa were together at the windmill. Red Cloud was a leader of the Sioux, and he and Papa were friends. He did not wear his hair loose to his shoulders as young Indians did. His black hair was in two long braids.

Susanna walked closer to the two men. They were
talking and did not see her. Red Cloud's eyes were
sad. Susanna knew why. Papa had told her. Red
Cloud had fought at the Battle of Wounded Knee
25 years ago. His wife and children had been killed
in the fight with the soldiers. The Sioux still called
it the Battle of the Hundred Slain.
They could not forget. And so
many settlers were still afraid of
Red Cloud and the other Sioux.

"In the <u>buffalo</u> days," Red Cloud said, "we were
happy here in our own country. The prairie was
full of four-legged game. The young men hunted.
We were never hungry, unless the winter was
long and the snow deep. Then the <u>Wasichus</u>
came. These settlers told us they wanted only a
little land. Enough to set a house on. But they
kept coming, like a river. They filled the prairie.
Their guns drove the buffalo far away. Now we
have little to hunt. Nothing to do. We must live on
a reservation, in a little pen. Our eyes run with tears."

"Wasichus" was a new word to Susanna. When Red Cloud rode away, she went to Papa. "What are Wasichus?" she asked.

"It means all of us," Papa said. "Settlers, home-steaders, soldiers." He told her that "Wasichus" means "They-are-too-many."

One afternoon Susanna went to the little creek on the prairie. She walked far along its bank and picked wild cherries. She heard a sound behind her and turned. She was looking right into the face of an old Indian. "Red Cloud!" she said.

"Little Yellow Fur!" he said.

Indian women and children came from the bushes. They carried skin bags of cherries. They laughed, happy to see her. "Come," they said. "Stay with us." Susanna was tired. She went with them. It was a long walk to their village. She could not keep up with the Indians. Red Cloud lifted her to his shoulders and carried her.

At last he put her down in a circle of tepees. Women bent over outdoor cooking fires. They turned roasts of rabbit and prairie hen. The meat smelled good. And Susanna was hungry. The women gave her bits of roast hen, which they called sheo. Boys and girls gathered around and ate with Susanna.

The cooking fires burned low. The sun went down. People yawned. Susanna was sleepy, too. She wanted to go home. But the prairie was dark. She did not know which way to go.

Red Cloud bent over her. His long black braids tickled her nose. She sneezed. "Come, Little Yellow Fur," he said. His spotted pony stood behind him. Susanna hoped he was going to take her home.

Suddenly a dog barked. A big bark. It sounded like Terk!

Then Papa came on his horse. Terk was with him.
Red Cloud lifted Susanna and put her in the
saddle behind her father. She put her arms around
Papa's waist and held tight. She was so glad to
see him. "I'm sorry if Susanna was any trouble,"
her father said to Red Cloud. Red Cloud spoke in
the Sioux language.

"Red Cloud wants you to come again," Papa said.

Red Cloud said to them, "In a Sioux village every
door is open to a child. Every pot has food for a
hungry boy or girl. Every heart loves children.
Helchetu aloh!"

Susanna knew "helchetu aloh" meant "It-is-true."
She felt happy.

Tortoise and Elephant

an East African folk tale
by Ruth Manning-Sanders

Tortoise was walking along a path through the woods when she met Elephant. Elephant said, "Tortoise, get out of my way or I will step on you."

That made Tortoise angry. She said, "What! You step on me? You couldn't step on me. I'd jump over your head!"

Elephant said, "You can't jump one inch."

Tortoise said, "I can jump! I can jump!"

Elephant said, "Well, let's see you."

Tortoise said, "No, I'm not going to jump today. I'm tired."

Elephant said, "Ha, ha, boaster! Now you're looking for excuses!"

Tortoise said, "No, I am not looking for excuses. Tomorrow let us meet here again. Then you'll see whether I can jump or not!"

Elephant said, "All right." And he walked off.

Next day Tortoise brought her sister to the meeting place. They looked as alike as two peas in a pod. She hid her sister under the bushes on one side of the path, and then she stood on the other side of the path. When Elephant came along, he didn't know there were two tortoises, one on each side of him. He could see only one.

"Oh, there you are, Tortoise!" Elephant said. "Well, are you going to jump?"

"Of course I'm going to jump," answered Tortoise. Tortoise made a little run. "Hupp!" cried she.

"Hey!" cried Tortoise's sister, coming out from under the bushes.

Elephant swung around. Could he believe his eyes? Yes, there was Tortoise on the other side of him! "Thousand thunders!" said Elephant.

"So you see I can jump," said Tortoise.

"Well, I have to <u>admit</u> that," said Elephant.
"I couldn't jump so high myself. But if it came
to racing now, I could really beat you."

"I don't know about that," said Tortoise.
"That will have to be proved. But I can't race
today because I've promised my cousins to have
dinner with them. Come here tomorrow and
I'll race you."

"All right," said Elephant. "We'll leave it till
tomorrow. We'll race to the foot of the hill
outside the woods."

132

Then Elephant went on his way. "I'll show her," he thought. "Boastful!"

Tortoise went out to dinner with her cousins. She had a great many cousins, and they were all exactly like Tortoise. She told them about the race and what she meant to do. They laughed and laughed.

That night they all went together to the woods. They hid all along the path—one here, the next farther on, and the next farther on still—, and the last one was at the foot of the hill. Oh, what a game! They were still laughing.

The next morning Tortoise was waiting. By and by along came Elephant. "Tortoise, are you there?"

"Yes, to be sure, I am!" Tortoise answered.

"Well then," said Elephant, "let's be off. Ready, set, GO!" Off went Elephant, running lightly, running fast. Tortoise didn't move.

Elephant ran and ran. Then he thought, "Tortoise must be a long way behind now!" And he glanced back over his shoulder. "Tortoise!" he called.

"Here!" cried a voice just ahead of him.

Elephant stared. Yes, there was Tortoise, in front of him! It was one of the cousins, you see, but Elephant couldn't know that. So on he ran, lightly and fast.

"Well, now I have left her far behind," he thought. And he glanced back over his shoulder. "Tortoise!" he called.

"Here!" cried a voice just ahead of him.

And there was Tortoise. "Thousand thunders!"
Who could believe it? Elephant ran on.

"Now I must have outrun her," he thought. And
he glanced back over his shoulder. Tortoise
wasn't even in sight! "Tortoise!" he called.
"Poor little Tortoise, I've really beaten you! Can
you hear me?"

136

"Hear you? I should think I could hear you!"
said Tortoise's voice just ahead of him.

Elephant stared. "Thousand thunders!
But I'll beat her. I will beat her!" thought
Elephant, and on he galloped. But every time
he looked around to see where Tortoise was,
there she was—just ahead of him. He ran faster
than he had ever run in his life, and when he
came to the foot of the hill, he was worn out.
"But I've won anyway," he thought.

Oho! Had he? Who was sitting waiting for
him but a tortoise? "I thought you were never
coming," said the tortoise.

So Elephant went slowly home. He was
hanging his head.

Then all the tortoise cousins went back to the
starting place. They laughed and laughed.
They danced around Tortoise, and she played
her flute.

A Small Discovery

by James A. Emanuel

Father,
Where do <u>giants</u> go to cry?

To the hills
Behind the thunder?
Or to the waterfall?
I wonder.

(Giants cry.
I know they do.
Do they wait
Till nighttime too?)

Hidden Ideas

If you saw a dog's wet, muddy footprints all over the kitchen floor, you would probably be right in thinking that a dog had been there. Not only that, you would probably be right again if you decided that the dog had been splashing in mud <u>puddles</u> before he came in. You didn't see the dog in the mud, and you didn't see him come in, but you knew what happened anyway. In the same way many times you get ideas from your reading that are not really written down. Learning to find these hidden ideas can help you be a better reader and have more fun reading, too.

Read the following story. Then answer the question that follows the story.

The man on the horse rode slowly in the hot sun. The grass and <u>shrubs</u> around him were dry and brown. The man and the horse were covered with dust. The man mopped his face with a cloth. Suddenly he saw the creek. With a <u>shrill</u> laugh the man splashed into the cold water. The horse began to drink.

Which of these ideas are hidden in the story?

1. It had not rained for a long time.
2. The man was very old.
3. The man and the horse had come a long way.
4. The horse was brown.
5. The man and the horse were hot and wanted water.

The Case of the Stolen Code Book

by Barbara Rinkoff

The new boy sat on his back porch steps watching the kids playing in the next yard. He knew their names, but they didn't know his. He had just moved in.

"Hi," he called and grinned at them over the bushes in the yard.

The girl called Winnie looked up, and her eyebrows slid under her Afro. But she didn't say, "Come and play."

The boys called John and Alex stopped arm wrestling and looked toward him. But they didn't say, "Come and play."

The smaller girl, called Holly, was sitting cross-legged next to her puppy, Panic. She gave a little wave and tossed her ponytail. But she didn't say, "Come and play."

The new boy watched Winnie take out a small black book.

"Meeting of the Secret Agents come to order," she said. She was a very businesslike girl.

And the new boy could tell they were having a club meeting. But no one said "Come and play" to him.

The Secret Agents were very busy using the small black book. The new boy wanted to see it, too. But whenever he tried to move from his porch steps, Panic barked.

When the kids left the yard, they forgot the small black book. So the new boy went over and picked it up. There was no name on the cover, so he opened the book. Inside it said SECRET AGENTS' CODE BOOK in big red letters. The new boy grinned. He liked codes. Then he had an idea.

Soon Winnie, Alex, John, Holly, and Panic came looking for the small black book.

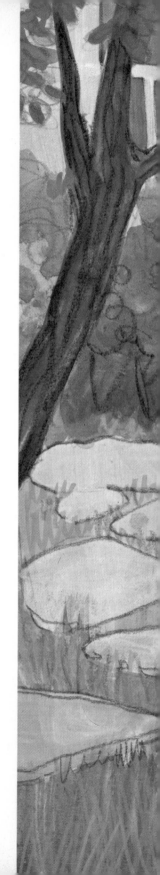

They searched all over, but all they could find was a blank piece of paper.

"Do you think it means anything?" Holly asked.

"Is it really blank?" asked Alex.

"Of course. I know writing when I see it, and I don't see it," said Winnie.

John grabbed the paper and whistled through his front teeth while he looked it over. Holly stood on tiptoe to look. Alex leaned closer and looked, too. Panic made a loud, noisy yawn.

"Nothing there. Nothing at all," said John.

"Unless it's in secret writing," said Alex.

"Secret writing?" the others said.

"Maybe it's a clue," said Alex, wiping his glasses clean on the tail of his shirt.

"A clue for what?" asked Holly.

"For our missing code book, of course," said Alex.

"How?" Holly wanted to know.

"Maybe the writing is invisible," said Alex.

"What's invisible?" asked Holly. She was always asking questions.

"You can't see it, dopey," said John.

"If you can't see it, what good is it?"

"Well, you can see it, if you know how," said Alex. He knew the most about magic and tricks.

"Then how?" asked Winnie, Holly, and John. "It's not in our code book."

Alex went to the garage and pulled the cord on the light hanging on the wall.

"You hold the paper next to the light," he started.

"I don't see anything," said Holly.

"There's nothing there. That's why," said John. And he began to whistle through his teeth again.

"Hey!" shouted Winnie. "The paper is burning!"

"Nope," said Alex. "Whoever left this note wrote it in milk."

"Are you trying to tell us a cow left it?" asked Winnie. She liked things to be clear.

"No," said Alex. "Someone left us this note written in milk, and to read it, we heat it with the light, and the writing will come out in brown letters."

And sure enough, there in front of them was a message. It said

To find
your book,
here's where
to look.
Try Panie's
favorite bed.

"Follow me!" called Holly, racing across the yard.

John poked his head and arm into the dog-house. Panic sniffed at his pants.

"Nothing there but an old bone," said John, throwing it across the grass.

Panic began to howl.

"Sh," said Holly.

"Sh," said Winnie, John, and Alex. "We're thinking."

"You sure this is Panic's favorite bed?" asked Alex.

"What other bed is there?" asked Holly.

"A flower bed?" said Winnie.

To the flower bed they ran, and, sure enough, there was Panic digging away.

"Here's something," cried John, holding up a folded piece of paper.

As he opened it, they all looked over his shoulder. It said

20-15   6-9-14-4   25-15-21-18   2-15-15-11
20-1-11-5   1-14-15-20-8-5-18   12-15-15-11
20-18-25   20-8-5   15-1-11

"Someone is using our code book," shouted Winnie.

"Let's try to figure out the message," said Alex. "Let's see. A is one. B is two. C is three."

"Oh, write it out or it will take all day," said Winnie.

She took out a paper and wrote

1 A	8 H	15 O	22 V
2 B	9 I	16 P	23 W
3 C	10 J	17 Q	24 X
4 D	11 K	18 R	25 Y
5 E	12 L	19 S	26 Z
6 F	13 M	20 T	
7 G	14 N	21 U	

And then they all read

TO FIND YOUR BOOK,
TAKE ANOTHER LOOK.
    TRY THE OAK.

"The oak tree!" Holly shouted. She led
the gang across the yard, Panic nipping
at their heels.

There, stuffed into a hole in the tree bark, was another note.

John opened the note. It looked very strange.

"What does THAT mean?" asked Holly.

"Search me!" said Winnie.

"What good would that do?" asked Holly.

"It could be one kind of mirror writing. Get me a mirror and I'll show you," said Alex.

Holly ran back to the house to get one.

"You stand the mirror in front of the letters, like this," said Alex. They all stood around him in the backyard watching him do it. Then they read

"Who's Bob Cox?"

Not one of them knew.

"I am," the new boy shouted across the bushes from his yard. "And here's your book." He held it out to Alex.

"Well!" said Winnie, Holly, and John.

"Not bad. Not bad at all," said Alex, and he smiled over his glasses as he took the code book.

"You took our code book!" the others said, pointing their fingers at Bob.

"I thought we could have some fun," he said.

Winnie, Holly, John, and Alex looked at each other. "How would you like to join our Secret Agents Club, Bob?" they all said together.

"You bet!" said the new boy, grinning his widest grin. "And you can have all my secrets for our code book!"

How Paul Bunyan
Beat the Mud an American folk tale

by Virginia Sprang

Paul Bunyan—the world's biggest, smartest, and strongest lumberjack—looked up at the sky. He was so tall he towered above the treetops. And something had just hit him on the nose. It didn't feel like rain. No, it was too thick. More and more of it was hitting his cap, his beard, and his great, wide shoulders.

"Ding-dang balderdash!" muttered Paul when he saw that it was mud.

Now Paul Bunyan wasn't too surprised by the mud rain. Weather in the wild northern woods could be strange at times. One winter the snow fell for weeks in great blue flakes. Paul remembered that winter well, for it was the year he found Babe, his blue pet ox. Yes, I said blue!

One windy night during the Blue Snowstorm, Paul had heard a loud, deep cry. He ran toward the lake and saw a blue head sticking out of the ice. Gently he tugged and pulled the animal toward the shore. He saw that it was a baby ox, but a big one — one that would grow to be as big and strong as Paul was.

The ox gave Paul a rough, wet lick of thanks. Paul laughed and said, "Well, seems I've got myself an ox! Think I'll call you Babe!"

Where Babe came from or how he got his blue color, Paul never knew for sure. Babe grew up to be his faithful friend and useful helper.

But to get back to the mud rain. Paul Bunyan and his men would be in big trouble if it kept up. For all the trees had been cut and the logs were piled high, waiting to be floated down the river to the sawmill. If the logs didn't get to the mill, there would be no pay for Paul and his men.

As the mud fell faster and thicker, Paul realized
that now any logs put in the river would be
stuck like toothpicks in a pot of molasses. Paul
had to do something, but what?

He thought and thought, and at last an idea hit
him. "Come on, Babe!" he yelled. "We've got
work to do!"

Paul packed his knapsack and set off in giant
strides across the land, with Babe close by his
side. They walked straight across the mountains
west to Coos Bay, the place where the whales
gathered. Paul knew about the whales because
a few years before he and Babe had worked
in the woods near Coos Bay and had gotten to
know the whales.

What did Paul have in mind? Some would say it was a crazy idea, but if you knew Paul, you knew it had to work. He and Babe went down to the shore, and soon the whales came to greet their old friends. Babe picked up a log with his jaws, swung it around, and flung it out into the water. The whales chased it and played with it, tossing it back and forth.

While Babe and the whales were playing, Paul dropped a huge net over the entrance to the bay and neatly fenced in the whales. "You know," said Paul to Babe, "our whale friends love mud, and they're just as good at swimming through it as through water."

So that was it! Paul was going to have a fleet of whales carry his logs to the mill!

Paul set right to work. He made bridles, reins, and packsaddles and got the whales used to them. In a few days Paul and Babe returned to camp with around three hundred whales.

Two mornings later the men at camp were blown out of bed by Paul Bunyan's loud shout, "ALL RIGHT, EVERYBODY OUT! Today the logs roll!"

The sleepy men pulled on their shirts and pants and went to the banks of the river. They rubbed their eyes because they couldn't believe what they saw. WHALES? With reins and packsaddles?

Then one man shouted, "Hooray! Let's get going!"

With roars of laughter and yells of joy, the men began piling the logs on the backs of the whales. Soon every log was loaded. "AWAY, ALL WHALES!" shouted Paul, and the strangest log float ever seen moved slowly but surely down the river of mud to the sawmill.

Is it any wonder that lumberjacks tell about Paul Bunyan and the Great Whale Log Drive to this very day?

Last Laugh

by Lee Bennett Hopkins

They all laughed when I told them
I wanted to be

A woman in space
Floating so free.

But they won't laugh at me
When they finally see
My feet up on Mars
And my face on TV.

Miguel's Mountain

by Bill Binzen

Miguel lives on a city street. He knows that street well, for he has never been out of the city. He has never seen a mountain.

One day Miguel's teacher read an old tale about a king who lived in a great castle high on a mountaintop. Miguel was so interested in the story that he didn't even know when the class was over. "I would love to climb a mountain!" he thought to himself.

Every day after school Miguel raced to the park down the block. The park was great fun! Miguel knew lots of boys and girls who played there.

163

One day some workmen came to the park. They
brought a steam shovel with them. They scooped
up dirt to make a hole for a new building. The hole
got deeper, and the dirt piled higher. Finally, the
workmen and their steam shovel went away.

That afternoon Miguel
went to the park as
usual. Some of his
friends were on the
huge pile of dirt.
Suddenly Miguel had
an idea.

He raced up, up, up to the top of the pile.
"It's a mountain!" he shouted. "It's a mountain,
and I'm the king of the mountain!"

In no time at all, that mountain was covered with
children. Up the mountain they ran, down and
around and around and up, all afternoon.

Every day after that more children were on the
mountain than anywhere else in the park.

Sometimes they would charge off it on wild
horses, and often they played cowboys. There
were blinding dust storms and games.

Then one day an alarming story spread through the park. Miguel couldn't believe it at first. Then he ran home as fast as he could, for he had to do something to keep back the tears.

For a long time he sat by the window, lost in thought. It was dark when his mother came home.

"What's the matter, Miguel?" she asked. "I've never seen you look so sad."

"In three days they're going to take away the mountain," Miguel answered. "They're going to take it away forever!"

Miguel's mother patted him on the head. "I know how you feel about that mountain," she said kindly, "but there's nothing we can do."

Miguel thought about the mountain long into the night. Suddenly he said to himself, "I've got an idea!" And he fell asleep at last.

Next morning before breakfast, with the help of his mother, he wrote this letter.

Dear Mr. Mayor,
Please don't let them take away the mountain in Tompkins Park. We children play on it every single day.
Love,
Miguel

He carefully addressed the envelope. On the front in big letters he wrote TO THE MAYOR, and on the back he put his own name and address.

Miguel knocked on the door of his friend Robert on his way downstairs. He told Robert all about the letter he had just written. The two boys raced off to the <u>post</u> office and carefully mailed the letter.

The next two days were very <u>difficult</u> for Miguel. It was hard to pay attention to his schoolwork. When the teacher asked him, "What is four and three?" he said, "Eight."

The third day was worse. On the third day the mountain would disappear forever.

After school Miguel walked slowly home. He took the long way because he couldn't bear to look into the park. He decided that he didn't want to go there ever again.

For a long time Miguel sat on the front steps of the house next door. He didn't feel like doing anything else.

Sometime later two extra-large feet appeared right under his nose. Miguel looked up.

A tall man with a friendly face was gazing down at him.

"Do you know Miguel García?" he asked.

"I'm Miguel García," Miguel said.

"Then you must be the boy who wrote the mayor a letter about the mountain," said the man.

"Yes, I am," Miguel said, feeling excited, though he wasn't sure why.

"Well," said the man, smiling, "I have good news for you, Miguel! You see, after the mayor read your letter, he had a talk with the man in charge of parks. They both agreed that your idea was a very good one.

"So they have asked me to tell you that your mountain will stay right where it is forever!"

170

At first Miguel couldn't say anything. But then his face lit up with the biggest grin the man had ever seen. Finally Miguel got his tongue back. "Thank you, mister," he said. "That's great news!"

Miguel raced off to the park. He forgot that only a few short hours before he had decided never to go there again.

"Great news! Great news!" he shouted. Soon all the boys and girls had crowded around him. Miguel told them everything the man had said.

As he finished, they all started talking at once.

"Let's have a parade to celebrate!" yelled Peter.

"Good idea!" everyone shouted.

And so it was arranged.

Tom brought a drum, and Ira brought a horn.
Carmen had a tambourine, and Eric brought his
big brother's trumpet.

What a time they had then! They paraded all
through the park, down every last path.

When they came to the top of the mountain,
everyone sang,

"Hooray for Miguel!
Hooray for Miguel!
He saved the mountain!"

It was getting dark, and slowly the boys and girls
went home one by one.

Early the next morning two small figures were seen racing to the top of the mountain. At the top they placed a flag.

"This really makes it official," said Eric. "From now on this will always be known as Miguel's Mountain."

Miguel didn't say anything. He just smiled.

174

Do You Write It or Say It?

What does the word **address** mean in the following sentence?

The mayor will address the city workers at a meeting tonight.

To find out, you probably need to look the word up in the Glossary. There you see that the word **address** appears like this.

> **ad dress** (ə dres´) to write on a letter
> where it is to be sent; to make a speech
> to   (ad´res or ə dres´) the place where
> someone gets mail

How can you tell which of the two meanings is the right one? If you think you should try out each meaning in the sentence, you are right. After you decide which meaning fits best in the sentence, write it down on your own paper.

Now read the first sentence that follows. Note the underlined word. Then look it up in the Glossary and decide which meaning best fits the sentence. Put the number 1 on your paper and after it write the meaning you picked. Do the same thing with the other sentences.

1. Jane drew the <u>figure</u> of a dog on her paper.
2. Tim has a new <u>gold</u> sweater.
3. There is a small lake in the <u>heart</u> of the woods.
4. Do you know how to <u>operate</u> the new dishwasher?
5. <u>Sign</u> your name at the top of your paper.

A <u>Garden</u> in Glass

by Bert I. Latossek

A garden growing in a closed or partly closed glass <u>container</u> is called a <u>terrarium</u>. The plants in a terrarium get along with one another. When they do this, they are in <u>balance</u> with each other.

It is fun to build a terrarium and take care of it. If you decide to make one of your own, here are the things you will need.

1. An empty jar with a neck that is big enough to put your hand through.

2. A few small pieces of charcoal. They can be bought at a plant store or a pet shop.

3. Some gravel or some small pebbles.

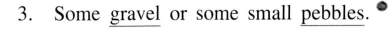

4. Any group of small weeds that are growing together in the backyard or anyplace near you. Dig out the plants with a spoon and keep some of the dirt around the roots to protect them. If you live in a place where there are no low-growing weeds, use seeds from apples, oranges, or grapefruit plus grass seeds or small clumps of grass.

5. Soil from a garden or from the place where you get the plants. Do not use very muddy soil unless you put sand with it.

Now that you know what supplies are needed, get them together and then begin your garden.

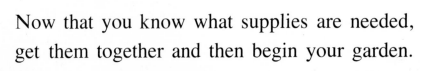

1. Stand your jar up if you want an upright garden, or put it on its side if you want a long garden.

2. Place the gravel or pebbles in the bottom of your garden.

3. Place the charcoal on top of the gravel or pebbles.

4. Cover the gravel or pebbles with a two-inch layer of soil. Make little mounds in your soil so your garden won't be flat.

5. Poke holes into the soil with your finger and then put the plants into the holes and cover their roots. Press the soil gently around the roots. If you are using seeds, just press them into the soil.

A terrarium needs lots of light, but it should not be in direct sun. To keep the plants in a glass garden healthy, water the soil only when it is almost dry. If any of your plants should get too large, trim them with scissors.

Collection 4

Words You Can Read

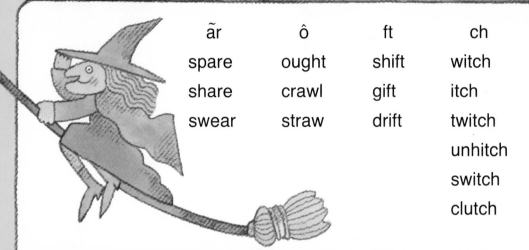

ãr	ô	ft	ch
spare	ought	shift	witch
share	crawl	gift	itch
swear	straw	drift	twitch
			unhitch
			switch
			clutch

they had	has not	he will	were not
they ha d	has n o t	he wi ll	were n o t
they'd	hasn't	he'll	weren't

begin	sleep	build	become
began	slept	built	became
begun	slept	built	became

Words You Can Read

adjective
amaze
attic
awaken
balcony
basement
Canada
Canadian
canary
carton
choir
clothing
cubbyhole
customer
dazzle
dispose
double
engine
errand
fiercely

glisten
guinea pig
handsome
instant
invitation
ironworker
limit
London
miserable
Mohawk
moment
Montreal
notice
owe
pigeon
politely
prefix
recipe
remain
repairs
repeat

reply
rubble
ruined
sheepish
silent
spaghetti
sparrow
stall
St. Lawrence River
suffix
Swedish
terrified
timid
treasure
trousers
tune
visit
volunteer
withdrew

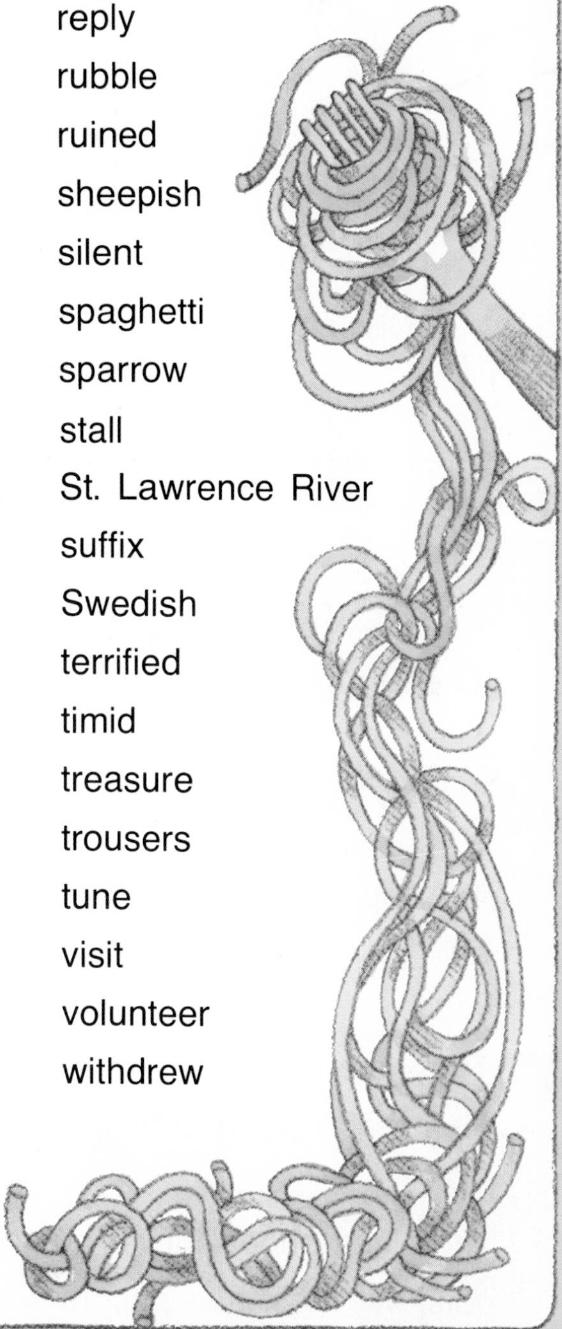

The Kippers Were Keepers

by Betty M. McCauley

The Kippers never threw anything—not anything—
out.

They kept bottles and string and <u>clothing</u> and bowls,
toys that were broken, and pans full of holes.

They kept shoes <u>they'd</u> outgrown, plants needing
pots, old rags, and papers with dog-ears and spots.

184

The children were Tommy, Sandy, and Ted. They
kept all their toys, from dollhouse to sled. And
they never threw anything ever away for fear they
might need it on some rainy day.

"These have a lot of good wear in them yet,"
said Mrs. Kipper as she stacked another pair
of Ted's raggedy <u>trousers</u> in her mending pile.
The pile covered all of the <u>spare</u> bed upstairs.

"And when I fix the sewing machine, it will be as good as new," said Mr. Kipper. "Then you can mend all those things." He started to look for his oil can, but he couldn't find it. "I'll have to build a tool chest for things like that some day—when I find my hammer and saw, that is."

"Don't worry about them," said Mrs. Kipper. "They are here someplace. It is so nice to have this big house with all the closets and drawers."

But the drawers were all filled with pencils and scraps and empty ink bottles and bent tacks and maps. And all the closets were filling up, too, with stacks of newspapers and magazines, old and new. Their clothes overflowed and were draped on the chairs and finally were shifted to closets downstairs.

"I really need to sort through those papers someday," said Mrs. Kipper as she pulled baby Tommy away from the desk. "There is a letter from Uncle John in there somewhere, and I really would like to read it again."

"Why don't we just ask Uncle John to come and visit instead?" asked Sandy. "He hasn't been here for a long time."

Sandy Kipper usually had good ideas, but this
was one of her very best! Right away Mrs. Kipper
looked in six drawers until she found the paper to
write an <u>invitation</u> on. Then Mr. Kipper took the
letter to the post office to buy a stamp because
they never did find any stamps in the drawers.
And last of all Mr. and Mrs. Kipper and Sandy
and Ted started to plan the weekend for Uncle
John.

"We'll have spaghetti for dinner when he comes," said Mrs. Kipper. She remembered that she had seen a recipe for spaghetti sauce in a magazine two years and three months ago, so Sandy said she would help find it. They looked through three stacks of magazines in closets and five under beds. But they couldn't find the recipe for spaghetti.

"That's all right," said Mrs. Kipper. "Uncle John likes canned beans just as well as we do."

"He can sleep in the spare bedroom," said Mr. Kipper. But then he remembered that the bed was covered with the stacks of mending that Mrs. Kipper must do some day—when he fixed the sewing machine.

"On second thought," he said, "Uncle John can sleep right here on the couch. It's comfortable." He moved three sweaters and a coat down to one end and sat down.

Mrs. Kipper said, "Uncle John brought you some toy cars last time he was here, Teddy."

"Toy cars!" cried Ted. "Where are they?"

Mrs. Kipper rubbed her chin. "I can't think just where now, dear," she said. "But I put them someplace where I'd be sure to find them when you were big enough to play with them."

"Is my sweater there, too?" asked Sandy. "I'm going to look for it so I can use it when Uncle John is here. He gave it to me."

"He gave me his picture," said Mrs. Kipper.

"Where is it?" asked Sandy. She looked around the walls.

"I've never seen it," said Ted.

"You haven't?" exclaimed Mrs. Kipper. "Well, I put it—I put it—I—don't remember where I put it." Mrs. Kipper folded her hands and unfolded them again. "We could look in the desk. It might be in the desk."

"Yes. Let's look in the desk!" said Mr. Kipper.

"We ought to have the picture on the wall when Uncle John comes," said Mrs. Kipper. "He wanted us to have it on the wall."

So Mrs. Kipper looked in the desk and the trunk, but she found only post cards and horseshoes and junk.

The girl and the boys and the mother and dad looked through the stacks and collections they had. From the attic to the basement they plowed all that day, finding stuff they'd forgotten they'd once put away. A lamp shade, a lamp wick, a string one inch long. Egg cartons, sea shells, one page of a song. But they looked, and they searched up and over and on without finding the picture of dear Uncle John.

"It's hopeless," said Mrs. Kipper. "He'll be disappointed, but we just can't find it."

"Too bad," said Mr. Kipper. "We simply can't find it."

The Kippers sat around and looked at each other. At least they could find each other. Mrs. Kipper wiped a tear off her nose. Mr. Kipper put his hands in his pockets and sighed. Ted sighed, too, and Tom cried because all of a sudden the Kippers, who were keepers, were not a very happy family.

But Sandy didn't sigh. Sandy didn't cry. Sandy
had an idea. She said in a timid voice, "We could
clean house."

"What did you say?" cried Mr. and Mrs. Kipper
and Ted.

"We could clean house," said Sandy, even more
quietly.

"How?" asked Mrs. Kipper.

"We could throw some magazines away," said Sandy.

"Oh, no!" Mrs. Kipper threw up her hands. "We
might read them someday!"

"And we could clean out the closets," said Sandy.

"Oh, no!" Mr. Kipper looked at the closet doors
that couldn't close. "Where would we put
everything?"

"Is it much work to clean house?" Ted asked quietly.

"Lots of work," said Sandy.

"Oh, too much work!" sighed Mrs. Kipper. "We could never do it. Uncle John will be so disappointed."

"He really will be," said Mr. Kipper. And he pushed his hands deeper into his pockets.

"I don't want Uncle John to be disappointed!" cried Sandy, standing up. "He's too nice to disappoint! I am going to start cleaning house myself!" She started out the door.

Ted followed. "Sandy," he asked, "would we find my toy cars if we cleaned house?"

"We'd find everything!"

"The spaghetti recipe?" asked Mrs. Kipper.

"Yes," said Sandy.

"And the oil for the sewing machine?" asked Mr. Kipper.

"Everything!" repeated Sandy.

Mr. Kipper looked at Mrs. Kipper, and Mrs. Kipper looked at Ted, and all three stood up. "Then we'll ALL clean house right now!" said Mr. and Mrs. Kipper and Ted. And Tommy sat down with a thump because he was so surprised!

They went out in the backyard for boxes galore
to dispose of the things they had wanted before.
Each did his share, and the job was begun. And
soon all the Kippers agreed it was fun. With a hip
hip hooray they were happy and gay, surprised it
was easy to throw trash away! Out went the
eggshells and papers and rags and five times five
boxes of stacked paper bags.

With the sewing machine oiled, Mrs. Kipper made
repairs on mending that covered the spare bed
upstairs. Clothes they'd grown out of were passed
down the line or given to someone who fit them
just fine. When the closets were cleared and the
chests straightened out, they all sang a song and
gave a cheer and a shout! And when they were
through, they still didn't mind, for what they had
left, they could use—and could find.

Three sheets full of stamps, all the missing door
keys. For sauce for spaghetti, thirteen recipes.
And down in a cubbyhole under the stair, all the
gifts Uncle John brought last time he was there.

Then back on a shelf where some scrapbooks were piled and clippings to paste in them someday were filed, Sandy found pictures. And there was the one for which the whole house-cleaning job was begun.

"Yippeeeee!" yelled Sandy and ran to show the others.

"Hooray!" cried Ted and Mr. and Mrs. Kipper. And Tommy hugged Sandy's knees because he wanted to see, too. Uncle John was a very handsome man!

198

Mr. Kipper hung the picture on the wall. Then Mrs. Kipper put fresh sheets on the bed in the spare bedroom. Ted and Tom played with the toy cars on the floor. The spaghetti sauce cooked in the kitchen. Sandy put her sweater on and hummed a happy little tune to herself.

When Uncle John came, he was pleased. And what's more, instead of only one day he stayed four. He noticed at once they had mended their ways. The Kippers weren't keepers again—for six days!

Two Witches

by Alexander Resnikoff

There was a witch.
The witch had an itch.
The itch was so itchy it
Gave her a twitch.

Another witch
Admired the twitch,
So she started twitching
Though she had no itch.

Now both of them twitch,
So it's hard to tell which
Witch has the itch and
Which witch has the twitch.

Joanna Runs Away

by Phyllis La Farge

Joanna loved animals. She loved Roger, her
gerbil. She loved Cleo, Rex, and Ruby, her
guinea pigs. She loved the animals in the zoo.
But more than any other animal Joanna loved
Costanza. Costanza was a horse. She pulled
Mr. Lauro's vegetable wagon.

Every Wednesday once spring came, Costanza came clip-clopping down Joanna's street. Joanna started waiting for Costanza the minute she was home from school. When she heard the horse's clip-clop, she took two lumps of sugar, the list her mother had made that morning before going to work, and the money her mother had left for her and went downstairs.

Joanna said hi to Mr. Lauro, but she did not
read him her mother's list right away. She waited
until all the other people had bought what
they wanted. That way she had plenty of time
to pat Costanza and to feed her the lumps of sugar.

Joanna liked Mr. Lauro. He was old. Her mother had told her that he was the last of his kind. Joanna wasn't sure what this meant. Maybe when he stopped coming around, no one would take his place. She hoped that he wouldn't stop because if he did, she would have no chance to see a horse. Costanza was the only horse she had ever seen.

When it was time for Mr. Lauro to go, Joanna always called, "See you next week."

Every Wednesday after Mr. Lauro had gone, Joanna felt sad. On other afternoons she played with Roger or with Cleo and Rex and Ruby. Sometimes she went downstairs to see the Martin family.

On Wednesdays Joanna just stayed by herself. She thought about what it was like to be all by yourself. It seemed to her that things would be better if she could live with Costanza. But when she thought about living with Costanza, Costanza was not pulling a vegetable wagon any more. Costanza and Joanna were in a green field, and the sun was shining.

One Wednesday, after Mr. Lauro had gone,
Joanna was sitting dreaming about Costanza
when there was a knock at the door. It was
Jimmy Martin. Joanna knew Jimmy felt all by
himself just the way she did. His big brother
played out in the street, and his twin sisters
were babies. Joanna knew Jimmy wanted her to
play with him, but he was younger than she was.

"Now I have an animal," Jimmy said. "I have a
turtle. And I have turtle food to feed it." He
was carrying the turtle in a plastic turtle dish.

"He's nice," Joanna said, "but turtles don't live long on turtle food."

"But this is good turtle food," said Jimmy. "My mother bought it for me at the store."

"I'm just telling you what my teacher told me," said Joanna. "Turtles don't live long on turtle food."

"They do so," said Jimmy. "This turtle is going to live forever." Then he ran out the door.

When he had gone, Joanna tried to think about Costanza again. But she couldn't. For the next few days, Joanna kept thinking about Jimmy, but she did not go to see him, and he did not come to see her.

Then Wednesday came again. It was a hot day. School was almost over. More than ever, Joanna wanted Costanza and Mr. Lauro to come. While she was waiting, Jimmy knocked at her door.

"What's good for turtles if it's not turtle food?" he asked. "My turtle is sick. Feel his shell."

Joanna touched the turtle's shell. It was very soft. Just then she heard Costanza's clip-clop. "I don't know," Joanna said. "I mean I can't tell you now. Costanza is coming."

Joanna grabbed her mother's list and the money and the sugar cubes and ran downstairs. Jimmy looked after her from the door of the apartment. "I'll wait for you," he called.

Joanna patted Costanza and fed her the sugar. "I'm glad to see you, Costanza," she said. "Are you glad to see me?" Then Joanna did a strange thing. Looking quickly this way and that, she climbed onto the wagon and hid under the frame that held the vegetables.

Mr. Lauro's scale rattled just a few inches from where she crouched. She thought maybe she should climb out, but she was afraid that someone would see her and ask her what she was doing. "I can always get out when he stops again," she thought. "Then people won't know me, and I can just go home."

But when Mr. Lauro stopped, there was never a moment when he or one or two of his customers were not standing at the end of the wagon.

And then the wagon did not stop any more.
Mr. Lauro just kept going. Clip-clop, clip-clop,
went Costanza's hooves. Each time they stopped
for a light, Joanna peered out the back of the
wagon and thought about jumping down. But she
didn't. Now they were traveling through parts of
Brooklyn she did not know. She was scared.

After a while there were no more big buildings,
just little houses with small yards around them.
"Pretty soon we will be in the country," Joanna
thought. She felt a lot better. "That's why I'm
here," she said to herself. "I'm going to find
Costanza a green field." But they rode on and
on, and the country never came.

At last the wagon stopped, and Mr. Lauro
jumped down. Joanna peeped out and saw him
open the doors of a shed. Costanza pulled the
wagon into the shed. Mr. Lauro unhitched her
and led her away. Then he began to lift the
boxes of vegetables and fruits off the wagon.

At last Mr. Lauro left the shed. All at once
Joanna wanted to be home. Was Mother
worrying about her? She felt the money and the
list in her pocket. How much time had gone by
since she left the house? Then she remembered
Jimmy. Was he still waiting for her? Maybe his
turtle was already dead.

Just then Costanza snorted quietly. Joanna
crawled down from the wagon. She found
Costanza in a stall at the back of the shed.
Joanna put her arms around the horse's neck.
She forgot about Jimmy.

She told Costanza that they were going to escape
together and look for the country. "We're going to
find a green place for you, Costanza," she said.

Joanna sat down on a heap of straw. She felt
sleepy. She stretched out comfortably on the
straw and drifted off to sleep.

When Joanna awakened, it was dark outside. She
did not know where she was. Then she smelled
the straw and smelled Costanza. She jumped
up. She opened the gate to Costanza's stall.
"Come on, Costanza," she said. "It's time to go."

Slowly Costanza followed Joanna. They
stopped at the door. Joanna peeked out. There
was no one in the yard. "OK, Costanza,"
Joanna whispered. "Let's go."

Clip-clop, clip-clop went Costanza's hooves. "Don't make so much noise, Costanza," whispered Joanna. "Ssh."

They passed alongside Mr. Lauro's house. "Hurry, Costanza," she said. "Let's get away from here."

But when they were a few feet from the sidewalk, Costanza stopped. Joanna tried to push her, but Costanza would not move another inch.

"Don't you want to be free?" Joanna whispered fiercely. "Do you want to stay in that hot old stall forever?"

Costanza stood for a moment longer. Then she swung around and headed back toward the shed. Clip-clop, clip-clop went her hooves. At that moment a light shone suddenly on the grass behind the house. Joanna heard Mr. Lauro say "Swear I heard that horse." Next thing he had seen them both.

"What's going on? Get back in your stall, old girl. And who are you?" Mr. Lauro grabbed Joanna and pulled her along with him while he drove Costanza back into the shed. He switched on the light and took a good look at Joanna.

"Aren't you the girl who always wants me to give my horse a drink?" he asked. Joanna nodded. "But what are you doing here? What are you doing with Costanza? You didn't think you could steal her, did you?"

"I wasn't trying to steal her," said Joanna. "I was trying to set her free. I was going to find a nice green field for her and me to live in."

Mr. Lauro began to laugh—a quiet laugh, not mean. "A green field?" he asked. "This is Brooklyn, and there haven't been any fields here in forty years."

"I know," said Joanna. "I wasn't really thinking. It was a sort of dream."

"And besides," said Mr. Lauro, "what would I do without Costanza? I'm an old man. I live by myself. Costanza is all I've got."

"I didn't think of that," said Joanna. "I didn't know you were all by yourself. So am I. I mean my mother works all day."

They went into Mr. Lauro's house and called
Joanna's mother. She sounded more worried
than mad. She said she would come right out,
but Mr. Lauro said he would bring Joanna
home. He hitched Costanza to the wagon. This
time Joanna rode up front, right next to
Mr. Lauro. The ride home was the most
wonderful thing that had ever happened to her.

"Don't run away again, kid," Mr. Lauro said.

"I wasn't running away," said Joanna. Then she
added, "Well, maybe I was."

When they reached her street, the Martin family,
some other friends, and her mother were
waiting for her. Her mother hugged her.

For a while Mr. Lauro stood around telling his part of the story. Then he said good-by to Joanna. "See you next week," he said.

"See you next week," Joanna replied. And then she went upstairs with her mother.

On the way up Joanna put her hand in her pocket. Her mother's list and the money were still there. She took them out. "I never bought what you wanted," she said. Her mother gave her another hug.

Then Joanna thought of Jimmy. She realized that he had not been out on the street when she arrived home. "I've got to see Jimmy," she said to her mother. "And I've got to buy him something."

"He was here when I came home," her mother said. "He was worrying about something." They went downstairs.

"Jimmy's mad at you," said Mrs. Martin. "He says you stood him up."

Joanna walked past Mrs. Martin into the back bedroom, where Jimmy slept with his big brother.

"Is your turtle still alive?" she asked. Jimmy nodded, but he didn't say anything.

"Fresh hamburger is what he needs and liver and lettuce. Cut up in little bits. That's what my teacher said. I'll help you get some tomorrow."

"You really will?" asked Jimmy.

"I really will," said Joanna. And then she went back upstairs with her mother and went to bed.

How Does Your Garden Grow?

Could you pick vegetables from your garden before you planted the seeds for them? Would you water the garden after you picked the vegetables?

Knowing or figuring out the right order in which to do things is often very important. Five sentences follow that tell the steps for growing a vegetable garden. The sentences are not in the right order. On a piece of paper write the number 1. After it write the sentence that tells what should be done first. Then write the number 2 followed by the sentence that tells what should be next. Go on to finish the list.

Eat the vegetables.
Water the growing plants and pull out the
    weeds around them.
Get turnip, squash, and carrot seeds.
Pick the turnips, squash, and carrots from the
    garden.
Plant the seeds.

Now do the same thing with the following seven sentences. These sentences tell a little story.

Mouse decided he would have to do something else that was special.

His teacher said, "Sure, Mouse. Come try out for the choir right now."

He asked his teacher if he could sing in the choir.

The teacher played another chord, but Mouse still squeaked.

But all he could do was squeak.

Mouse wanted to do something special.

The teacher played a chord on her guitar, and Mouse tried to sing.

The Mohawk Skywalkers

by Carol Thorpe

When you look down from a high place, do you get a funny feeling inside? Do you get dizzy and scared? Most people do. But the people who build skyscrapers have learned not to be scared. They know their work is dangerous, but they also know how to be careful.

Although people of all backgrounds work on these big buildings, some Mohawk Indians can be found working on almost all of them. The story of how the Mohawks got started as "high iron-workers" begins many years ago near the St. Lawrence River, close to Montreal, Canada. The Mohawks and four other tribes lived there. They farmed, fished, and hunted on the land they loved. Many still do.

But in 1886 the Canadians decided to build a bridge over the St. Lawrence River near the Indians' home. It was to be a very high, very long bridge. The people planning the bridge needed workers who were brave enough to work very high over the river with the cold wind whipping about them. But where could they find such workers? Since this was before any skyscrapers had been built, there were no high ironworkers yet. The planners found some sailors who were used to climbing the high riggings of ships and were willing to try. There were not enough sailors, but work was begun anyway. Soon some of the beams were in place, and part of the bridge began to take shape.

One day one of the workers on a high beam turned around and was surprised to see one of the Mohawk men standing behind him. The Indian's name was Jim Talking Wind. "I want to work," he said with a grin.

"You're not scared to be up here?" asked the worker.

"Scared? No! What of?" was Jim's answer. He laughed at the <u>amazed</u> look on the man's face.

Soon many Mohawks were working on the bridge, walking along the sky-high beams as though they had been doing it all their lives. They liked the work, they were very good at it, and they were paid well for it, too.

When the bridge was finished, some of the Indians moved on to New York City, where some tall buildings were beginning to go up. Because of their special ability and their experience on the bridge over the St. Lawrence, the Mohawks easily got jobs working on the skyscrapers. Ever since then some Mohawk Indians have been high ironworkers.

Today if you live in or visit a big city and you see a very tall building going up, there's a good chance that some of the workers walking along the beams hundreds of feet in the air are Mohawk Indians.

One businessman who works in a large city and is a Mohawk Indian said with a grin, "You know, whenever I pass a skyscraper going up, I look up and yell WHOO-HOO-HOO!" He sounded just like an owl. "If I get a WHOO-HOO-HOO back, I know one of my Mohawk brothers is up there somewhere!"

Charley, Charlotte, and the Golden Canary

by Charles Keeping

Here on Paradise Street, somewhere in the big city of London, lived two children called Charley and Charlotte.

They were great friends, and every day they played together on Paradise Street.

Most of all they liked to look in the stores on Paradise Street—especially the pet store, with its kittens and puppies and the little golden canary that sang and sang in its cage. Charlotte and Charley used to sit on the steps of an old building near the pet store and feed the pigeons and sparrows that came down in search of food.

Then one day everything changed. Workers came to tear down the old houses on Paradise Street, and Charlotte's house was the first to go.

Charlotte and her mother went to live in an apartment at the very top of a brand-new building. Because the building was so high and the street far away below, Charlotte's mother no longer allowed her to go out to play.

From their little iron balcony Charlotte could look down and see the stores on Paradise Street. But she never once saw Charley. She felt very lonely and missed her friend.

Down on Paradise Street Charley also felt lonely and <u>miserable</u>. He was not even sure where Charlotte lived now. All the new buildings looked alike.

He would stand in front of the pet store and look at the golden canary, thinking all the time of Charlotte.

The buildings of Paradise Street were slowly turning into piles of bricks and junk. Soon only the pet store <u>remained</u>. Charley <u>became</u> so lonely that he decided that if he could not have Charlotte's friendship, he would have to have the next best thing—the golden canary.

He ran to the pet store. "Please, Mr. Finch, how much do you want for the golden canary?" he asked.

"Well," said Mr. Finch, "suppose you work hard for a couple of weeks. Then maybe you will have enough money to buy the bird."

Charley set to work right away. He collected heaps of papers, bottles, rags, and old scrap for Junky Slatter, the junk dealer.

Then for a few days Charley helped Dick Johnson, a cleaning man. And he took dogs for walks.

Then he ran errands and collected firewood from the ruined houses in an old baby buggy.

After two weeks of very hard work, he took his money to Mr. Finch.

Kind Mr. Finch not only sold Charley the canary, but gave him the canary's cage as well. Charley walked proudly away, clutching his treasure.

All of this time Charlotte played alone on her balcony. Her mother was very busy and could not take her out very often.

Charley loved his little golden bird. But he was still lonely, for although it could sing, it could not talk or play with him. Charley often told his bird about Charlotte and the games they used to play.

One day Charley took the canary's cage out into the backyard to clean it. He opened the small wire door and slowly put in his hand to get the canary. Unknown to him, a stray cat was watching from the fence.

Because the little canary trusted him, it settled on Charley's finger.

Gently Charley withdrew his hand from the cage. At that very instant the cat sprang!

Terrified, the golden canary flew away. Up, up, up it soared.

The bird's wings glistened against one of the brand-new apartment buildings.

Charley scrambled over the wooden fence and ran through the rubble to the apartment building.

The great building towered above him. He strained his eyes against the <u>dazzle</u> of the sun.

Suddenly his heart leaped for joy! High above him he could see his old friend Charlotte waving her hand to him.

Charley rushed up hundreds of stairs until he arrived, panting, at the top. There stood Charlotte, and — believe it or not — perched on her finger was his little golden bird!

After that everything was happy. Charlotte's mother said that Charley could come over whenever he liked. So every day he came to play with Charlotte on her balcony high above Paradise Street, and he often took the golden canary that had helped him find her again.

PAPER I   Paper is two kinds, to write on, to wrap with.
If you like to write, you write.
If you like to wrap, you wrap.
Some papers like writers, some like wrappers.
Are you a writer or a wrapper?

by Carl Sandburg

PAPER II   I write what I know on one side of the paper
and what I don't know on the other.
Fire likes dry paper and wet paper laughs at
fire.
Empty paper sacks say, "Put something in me,
what are we waiting for?"
Paper sacks packed to the limit say, "We hope
we don't bust."
Paper people like to meet other paper people.

by Carl Sandburg

234

The Day Taku Smiled

by Miyoshi Izui

Mieko was walking down the dusty road from the
schoolhouse when she saw something glistening
in the sun. She stooped to see what it was and
picked up a piece of beautiful blue green glass.
The edges had been worn smooth by the stones in
the road. "Maybe," thought Mieko, "this will make
Taku smile." She slipped the glass into her pocket
and ran the rest of the way home.

Taku was Mieko's little brother. He had been in the hospital in the city for a long time. Mr. and Mrs. Takada had brought him home thinking that he would soon be running around and shouting with the other five-year-olds on their street. But Taku didn't get any better. He didn't eat much or say much, and he always looked sad.

One day Mieko heard her mother say to her father, "If only he would WANT to get well! If only we could do something to make him happy. I'd give anything in the world to see him smile again!"

Mieko was worried about Taku, too. She had spent every extra minute trying to make Taku smile. She had brought him funny things and pretty things. She had made pictures for him. And she had done double backward somersaults for him and learned how to balance a cane on the end of her nose. Taku had not laughed or even smiled. But Mieko did not give up.

After dinner that night Mieko gave him the beautiful blue green piece of glass she had found. Taku put it into the box in which he kept the things he liked. "Thank you, Mieko" was all he said. Mieko was disappointed.

Next morning a wonderful idea came to her. She hurried through her breakfast. Then she excitedly dashed out of the house and ran to the Street of Shops. She went straight to the shop of Mr. Sakamoto, who, besides selling yards of silk and flowered cloth, was also the chief of the town's volunteer fire department.

Mieko made herself wait <u>politely</u> till Mr. Sakamoto
came over to where she was standing.

"And what can I do for you, Mieko?" he asked in
his booming voice.

Mieko made a little bow and started right in.
"Mr. Sakamoto, I wonder if you could do something
for my little brother, Taku."

"And what might that be?" asked Mr. Sakamoto.

Mieko told him her idea. Mr. Sakamoto listened
thoughtfully as she talked. He was <u>silent</u> for a few
moments after she finished, and then he said,
"Well, Mieko, it's very unusual. But I don't see any
real reason why it can't be done. How about next
Sunday?"

Mieko felt like a flying bird as she ran home. Later when Taku was asleep, she told her mother and father about her visit with Mr. Sakamoto. They were a little surprised by her boldness but pleased with her unusual plan.

At about one o'clock on the next Sunday, there was a loud noise in the street outside Mieko and Taku's house. What could it be? Taku peeked outside. His eyes grew wide. There in front of his house, with Mieko in the front seat next to the driver, was the town's beautiful bright yellow fire engine. Mr. Sakamoto had on his fancy fireman suit with bands of gold in his hat. He was bowing and waving to the gathering crowd. Mieko jumped down and ran into the house.

"Come on, Taku!" she yelled. "We've come to get you. You're going for a ride on the fire engine!"

Taku looked at Mother. She laughed and nodded yes. She bundled up Taku in a warm sweater, and Father carried him out to the engine. Everyone cheered as Taku was placed in the seat of honor.

Then Mr. Sakamoto started the motor, and the
engine started very slowly down the street.
"Errrrrrrrrrrr," said the siren. "Clang! Clang!" went
the bell.

Taku's eyes twinkled with excitement. Then he
couldn't help it. A great big smile spread over his
face. Mieko, who was running alongside the engine,
was very pleased that finally her brother was happy.

The engine made its way down Taku's street, up to the Street of Shops, past the town hall to the edge of town, and back again. When they got back to Taku's house, Mother invited Mr. Sakamoto into the house for some sweet bean-paste cakes and tea. Grandfather, Grandmother, and old Aunt Yuri had come, too. And the visit turned into quite a party. Taku kept right on smiling and ate four sweet cakes, much to his mother's surprise.

When Mr. Sakamoto was leaving, he said to Mieko, "Mieko, don't worry. I know Taku is going to get better. He asked me if he could have my job on the fire engine when I get too old to work! That was a very good idea you had!"

Now it was Mieko's turn to smile.

The Word Changers

The pictures show members of the **appear** family.
What do the underlined prefixes **dis** and **re** mean when
added to the word **appear**?

appear

Did you figure out that the prefix **dis** means "the
opposite of," and the prefix **re** means "again"?
The prefix **re** can also mean "back." If you owe
someone something and you want to pay the person
back, what do you do? You repay that person.

disappear

Just as prefixes can give clues to the meanings of
words, many suffixes can tell how words are used
in sentences. If you add the suffix **ish** to the noun
sheep, you get **sheepish**. How would the word be
used in a sentence? Before you answer, think
about this sentence.

Pat's puppy had a sheepish look on its face
after it ate the cat's food.

Did you decide that the suffix **ish** added to a noun
makes a word that is an adjective?

reappear

The suffix **ish** can also be added to the name of a people to tell about their language or something they make or do. For example, a Swede speaks Swedish and makes Swedish pancakes. What language does a Dane speak?

Now get a piece of paper. Add the prefix **dis** to a word you know. Use the word you make in a sentence. Add the prefix **re** to a word you know and write a sentence with that word in it. Write **again** or **back** after your sentence to show what the prefix means.

Next, add **ish** to the words **green** and **child**. Use the words you make in sentences.

Add **ish** to the words **Turk** and **Finn** and use these words in sentences.

Now write a sentence or two explaining why prefixes and suffixes could be called word changers.

Collection 5

Words You Can Read

selfishly = self + ish + ly
dreamily = dream + y + ly
angrily = anger + y + ly

unforgivable = un + forgive + able
uncovered   = un + cover + ed
uncarpeted = un + carpet + ed

American = America + an
Italians = Italy + an + s
Mexicans = Mexico + an + s
Africans = Africa + an + s

one hoof ⟶ two hoofs

or

one hoof ⟶ two hooves

kneel   sweep   expect   enjoy
knelt   swept   expected   enjoyed

Words You Can Read

aluminum	fantastic	pollution
appointed	favor	principal
approval	fizzle	rear
audience	garbage	romp
auditorium	grace	Schenectady
booklet	helicopter	seize
capital	hind	self-confidence
catalog	Illinois	separate
centipede	Japanese	Spain
Chicago	Kentucky	spectator
compost	kimono	sprawl
dashiki	Ms.	superintendent
deliver	niños	support
district	opinion	surpass
drizzle	original	taco
ecology	pail	talent
electric	performance	teakettle
electricity	personal	twirl
engineer	phrase	wander
entertain	plead	windowpane

A Teacher's Teacher
by Knapp Willson

Did you ever wonder what a doctor does when she or he can't figure out what's the matter with someone? Or what a baseball pitcher does when the ball just isn't going over the plate? If you thought that the doctor goes for help to another doctor and that the pitcher goes to the coach, you were right.

But where do you suppose your teacher and <u>principal</u> go when they need help? They go to a teacher's teacher—a very special kind of coach!

The large picture at the far left shows Dr. Rhodes working with a third-grade reading class. The small picture on this page shows her listening to the children.

In one school district in <u>Illinois</u> the teacher's teacher is Dr. Bessie Rhodes. There are twenty schools in her <u>district</u>, so Dr. Rhodes is very busy. But wherever she goes, there's a smile on her face and a bounce in her walk. For Dr. Rhodes loves teaching and children and teachers and principals. And she loves helping them.

Dr. Rhodes not only teaches, she also learns on her job every day. Teachers, principals, other teacher's teachers, and even children help her learn. "Some of my very best ideas about how children learn come from children themselves," Dr. Rhodes explains. What she learns she shares with the principals and other teachers in the school district.

Dr. Rhodes does many other important things. She likes being an all-around helper. And she's almost always on call. If, for example, a teacher wants help in setting up a room library for a study of the city where the children live, Dr. Rhodes will help find the right maps, booklets, and films. She may even ask an older man or woman who has lived in the city for a long time to come to the class and tell about the city.

The picture at the far left shows Dr. Rhodes and the children getting into a discussion about classifying. The next picture shows Dr. Rhodes giving special attention to one of the boys.

"Going into a classroom and working with children is another thing I love to do," says Dr. Rhodes. And she does it often. For example, when new reading books are being used for the first time, Dr. Rhodes will teach a reading class seven or eight times. The room will be crowded, for in it there will be children plus reading teachers and principals who are on hand to find out how to teach with the new books.

The children's reading teacher, shown at the far right, pays attention, too, as Dr. Rhodes and the pupils continue their lesson.

The pictures at the left and above show
Dr. Rhodes and the children working
together. They enjoy her as much as
she enjoys them. Below at left Dr.
Rhodes is shown talking to a school
principal, and at right she is seen
meeting with the superintendent of
the school district.

At the right Dr. Rhodes stops in
the school hall to answer some
last-minute questions of the
reading teacher whose class
Dr. Rhodes worked with earlier.

252

"It gives me such great joy to work with children who are learning to read," Dr. Rhodes says with a grin. "Even when I was a principal, I taught reading every day just because I liked it so much."

"I have been learning how to be a teacher all my life," Dr. Rhodes goes on. "When I was growing up in Kentucky, I played school every chance I got. And I always had to be the teacher! Even when I was alone, I practiced teaching. You should have seen me teaching all my toys and all the neighborhood cats and dogs!"

Dr. Rhodes learned a lot about teaching from her father. He was a teacher and later a principal. At times when Dr. Rhodes was growing up, she didn't like being the "teacher's kid." Sometimes the other children thought that she had things easy or that she might tell her father about what they did. None of it was true, but it hurt to know the children felt that way. Dr. Rhodes hoped her own children would never have to go through that.

So when her son, Robbie, was ready for third grade in the school where she was a third-grade teacher, Dr. Rhodes made sure he was not in her room. Robbie says, "At first I wanted to be in my mom's class. But later I was sure glad I wasn't. Mom was right. She knew just what to do."

Above Dr. Rhodes talks to her son, Robbie, about his clarinet playing. At the right Robert Rhodes joins his wife and son for a baseball game in the park.

The teachers and principals who work with Dr. Rhodes agree with Robbie. Dr. Rhodes usually seems to know just what to do. Or if she doesn't, she knows how to find out. She's a great coach and problem solver. No problem is too big or too little for her. The teachers and principals know that all they have to do is ask.

The Horse Who Could Do Almost Anything

by Lois Sorkin

One day a horse who had many unusual talents wandered into strange fields. There he saw other horses running together, and he wanted very much to make friends with them.

The other horses didn't seem too friendly, and he soon realized that he would have to make the first move.

257

He said to them, "I can do many interesting things. Meet me tomorrow by the big shade tree when the sun is straight above, and I'll show you." And he galloped away to practice a trick.

The next day the others were waiting at the appointed place at the appointed time. He stood before them with grace and self-confidence. As they watched closely, he reared up and clapped his front hoofs together—which for a horse is amazing.

"Very interesting," they said and nodded their approval. Then the little group broke up, and they seemed to be going their separate ways again.

"Wait! I can do other tricks, too. Meet me tomorrow by the corner of the fence when the sun is straight above, and I'll show you." And he trotted off to practice.

The next day his audience was waiting at the appointed place at the appointed time.

This time he did an even better trick. He stood on one <u>hind</u> leg and balanced himself — which for a horse is amazing.

"Most unusual," they said, nodding their approval.

"But wait! I can do more tricks! Meet me tomorrow by the side of the grassy hill when the sun is straight above, and I'll show you." And off he went to practice.

The next day the little group met at the appointed place at the appointed time.

The talented horse stood before them, balanced himself on his front legs, and walked several steps—which for a horse is amazing.

The spectators nodded their admiration.

"Quite clever," they all agreed. And they returned to the fields to romp and run.

"Wait!" pleaded the horse. "I will do an even better trick tomorrow. Meet me by the little pebbly stream when the sun is straight above, and I will show you."

And they did. This time the horse outdid himself.
He stood on his nose and twirled his body—
which for a horse is amazing.

The other horses gasped. "Truly fantastic," they
all said. "And what will you do for us tomorrow?"

"Why, it will be a surprise," he told them. "Meet
me tomorrow on the top of the mountain when
the sun is straight above." And off he trotted.

But he was worried. "What can I do?" thought the horse. "How can I surpass what I have already done? Of course, I could run away and they'd never find me, but still I would not have their friendship. No, I'll stay. But what—what can I do?"

The next day the horse appeared at the appointed place at the appointed time. "Today I am going to do the hardest trick of all. I'm going to show you what fools we've all been. And I've been the silliest fool of all."

The horses looked at him oddly. This was not what they had expected to hear.

"Each day you have all come out here selfishly trying to amuse yourselves. Did any of you once try to be kind to the one who has given you pleasure? No!

"And I, I am the most foolish of all. I tried to gain your friendship in a most unforgivable way. I have been nothing but a show-off."

He turned sadly away from them and began to make his way down the mountain. Suddenly, in the background, he began to hear hoofbeats.

"Stop!" called one of the horses.

He turned and saw that they were all there.

"You were right," said another. "We have been both foolish and selfish. We do not want you to entertain us any more. We want you to like us. We want you to be our friend."

The others nodded in agreement, and then all trotted together to the new fields.

And the talented one taught them all something important—which for a horse is amazing.

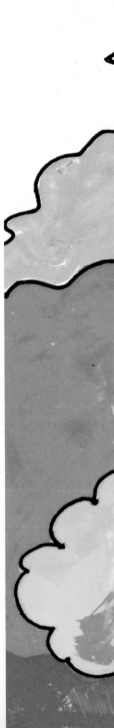

Old Words and New

The language we speak is filled with words. Where do these words come from?

Some words are very, very old. Among them are words like **love** and **truth**. Others are words for everyday things, like **cat** and **house**. Many old words are words that glue sentences together—for example, **and**, **when**, **to**, **at**, **with**, and **but**. Here is a sentence made of words that have been in our language for more than one thousand years.

The girl and her dog live in the woods.

Some words are made up to name new things. When your grandmother's mother was young, she never heard the word **movie** because moving pictures had not been invented. And when your grandmother was a girl, she didn't know the word **nylon** because no one had yet created this very useful material.

Old things that already have names are sometimes given new names. And both names are used. This makes the language richer. For example, the **helicopter** is now often called a **chopper**.

When we start using something from another people, we often borrow the name as well as the thing. When we got **squash** from the American Indians, **spaghetti** from the Italians, **tacos** from the Mexicans, the **dashiki** from the Africans, and the **kimono** from the Japanese, we called them by their original names.

Now look at this.

Make up a name for it. Next, think up another name for a TV set. Then see if you can think of something borrowed from another land that we call by its original name.

Friday Night Is Papá Night

by Ruth A. Sonneborn

Pedro sat on the kitchen floor, pushing two little cars around and around.

"Is tonight Friday night, Mamá?" he asked.

"Yes," Mamá said. "Tonight is Friday night."

Pedro clapped his hands. "Papá is coming. Papá is coming," he sang. "Papá comes every Friday, doesn't he, Mamá?"

Mamá nodded her head.

"Mamá," he said, "why doesn't Papá come home every night? Ana's papá comes home every night. Why not my papá?"

Mamá sighed. "Poor Papá," she said, "has to work very hard. He has to have two jobs to get enough money so we can eat and have a place to live. His jobs are far from here, too. Poor, poor Papá. He works so hard."

The door opened, and Manuela, Carlos, and Ricardo came in together from school.

"Tonight is Friday night," Pedro shouted. "Papá is coming."

"Who doesn't know that, silly?" Carlos said.

"Never mind the talk," Mamá said. "We have work to do. Everyone gets a job."

By late afternoon the jobs were done, and the table was set. The kitchen was filled with smells that made everyone hungry.

Pedro went to the window. He stared down into the street. It was beginning to grow dark.

"I don't see Papá," he said.

Manuela looked at the kitchen clock. "He's awfully late already, Mamá," she said. "What could have happened?"

"Don't worry," Mamá said. "Papá will come."

"Yes," Pedro said. "Papá always comes on Friday." He pressed his face against the windowpane. "Look," he said. "The street lights are on now. Where is Papá?"

They waited and waited.

Finally, Mamá went to the stove.

"Come, niños," she said. "We must eat. Papá will come while we eat."

The children came to the table. No one talked.

Then Pedro said, "I don't want any supper. I want Papá."

Pedro got up from the table and crawled onto his bed, which was in a small room next to the kitchen. He put his head on his pillow. Mamá came over. She covered him with a blanket.

"OK, Pedro," she said. "Go to sleep now."

Pedro sat up. "No, no, no," he shouted. "I don't want to sleep. I want to wait for Papá."

Mamá hugged him. "Go to sleep now, Pedro," she said. "I will wake you when Papá comes."

"Sure?" Pedro asked. "Promise?"

"Promise," Mamá said.

Pedro's eyes closed.

Suddenly Pedro woke up. He opened his eyes. The kitchen was very dark and empty. There was just one spot of light on the floor by the window.

Pedro sat up in bed.

And then he remembered.

Papá. Papá had not come home.

There on the kitchen table was Papá's plate, his fork, his knife, his spoon, his glass, his napkin—still on the table. All clean and unused.

Pedro got out of bed and ran to the window. He looked down into the street. A noisy car drove by. Two people walked past.

Where was Papá? Why hadn't he come home?

Pedro pulled a chair over to the window. He knelt on it and stared into the street. There was no one there. Then a cat ran across the street. A policeman walked slowly past.

He saw a dark shadow moving. The shadow moved closer. Was it? Yes, it was a man. It was a man carrying a fat shopping bag. Papá always brought a fat shopping bag home with him. The man came closer. Papá! Pedro was sure it was Papá.

He hurried across the kitchen and turned on the light. The kitchen now looked brighter than day.

He ran to the door and opened it wide.

"Papá," Pedro shouted. "Papá, you're here."

He hugged Papá, and Papá hugged him.

In another minute Mamá, Manuela, Ricardo, and Carlos came running from their beds.

"Papá, Papá, what happened?" everyone asked at the same time.

"What happened?" Papá said. "I'll tell you what happened. My friend Juan who works with me got sick. I took him to the hospital. Then I went to tell his wife. I couldn't get home sooner. You understand, niños?"

"We should have a phone," Carlos said. "Everyone else has a phone."

"I know, but a phone costs money," Mamá said. She took Papá by the hand. "Come, sit down. You must be very tired."

Papá sat down. "You know," he said, "coming home now I was so tired. So very tired. I looked up at the window. It was dark. I thought, now I have to climb the stairs. Now I have to go into a dark apartment. Everyone will be sleeping. No one will be at the door to meet me. But suddenly there was a light in the kitchen window. Someone was up. Someone was waiting. And"—he pulled Pedro onto his lap—"it was my Pedro. My Pedro had turned on the light. My Pedro was at the door waiting for me. And suddenly I was not tired any more."

Papá hugged Pedro and set him down on the floor. He drew the fat shopping bag toward him.

"Come now," he said. "Let's begin." He dipped his hand into the bag.

"Popsicles," the children shouted. Papá always brought Popsicles.

"Popsicles in the middle of the night?" Mamá said. "Whoever heard of Popsicles in the middle of the night?"

Papá dug again into the shopping bag.

He handed out sneakers for Pedro, a blouse for Manuela, socks for Carlos, pajamas for Ricardo, and to Mamá he gave one red rose.

"It's just like Christmas when Papá comes home," Pedro said. "Just like Christmas."

Mamá heaped Papá's plate with fish and beans, and everyone sat around the table talking, laughing, watching Papá eat.

"Yes," Pedro said <u>dreamily</u>, "Friday night is the nicest night. Friday night is Papá night."

A Song to Sing to Some Raindrops

by Bobbi Katz

Soft rain,
spring rain,
drizzle drip and sing rain!
Dance rain,
dream rain,
fizzle skip and drip rain!
Splish rain,
swish rain,
ice cream in a dish rain!

Uncle Mitya's Horse

by Leo N. Tolstoy

Uncle Mitya had a fine horse. He kept it in a pen that had a fence around it. But some thieves found out where he kept his horse and planned to steal it from him.

Now it happened one night that a farmer came to visit Uncle Mitya and brought his pet bear with him. So Uncle Mitya let the horse out into the yard and put the bear in the pen where the horse had been.

In the dark the thieves came creeping. They
stole up into the pen. But they found no horse
there! What they found was that great big bear.
The bear seized one of the thieves, and how the
fellow screamed! He screamed so loud Uncle
Mitya heard him. Then Uncle Mitya and the
farmer ran from the house and caught the
thieves.

Maxie

by Mildred Kantrowitz

Maxie lived in three small rooms on the top floor
of an old brownstone house on Orange Street. She
had lived there for many years, and every day was
the same for Maxie.

Every morning, seven days a week, every morning
at exactly seven o'clock Maxie raised the shades
on her three front windows. Every morning at
exactly 7:10 Maxie's large orange cat jumped up
onto the middle window sill and sprawled there in
the morning sun.

At 7:20 if you were watching Maxie's back window, you could see her raise the shade to the very top. Then she uncovered a bird cage. On the perch inside the cage was a yellow canary. He was waiting for his water dish to be filled, and it always was, if you were still watching, at 7:22.

At 8:15 every morning Maxie's door opened with a tired squeak. Maxie's old leather slippers made slapping sounds as she walked down the four flights of uncarpeted stairs to the front door. Outside the front door were the bottles of milk that had been delivered. Maxie always tried to hold the door open with her left foot while she reached out to get her milk. But every morning it was just a little too far for her to reach. The door always banged shut and locked behind her.

So at 8:20 every morning Maxie rang the bell marked "Superintendent." The superintendent, whose name was Arthur, would open the door for Maxie and let her in with her milk.

Only Maxie and the man at the grocery store knew what she ate for breakfast, but everyone knew she drank tea. At 8:45 every morning they could hear the whistling of her teakettle. How Maxie loved that whistle! She loved it so much that she let it sing out for one full minute. Dogs howled, cats whined, and babies bawled, but everyone knew that when the whistle stopped, it would be 8:46. And it always was.

The mailman knew more about Maxie than anyone else did. He knew that she had a sister in Chicago who sent her a Christmas card every year. He also knew when Maxie planted the flowers in her window boxes because every spring he delivered her seed catalog. Then a few weeks later he delivered packets of seeds.

Every morning at nine o'clock Maxie walked down
the stairs for the second time in her leather
slippers. She went outside and put her small bag
of <u>garbage</u> in the <u>pail</u> on the front stoop. Then she
came back in and waited for the mailman. She
walked slowly past him in the hall, watching him
put mail in the slots for the other people who lived
in the house.

Then she climbed the four flights of stairs again,
resting at each landing. When she got to the top,
Maxie went into her apartment, and the door
closed after her with the same tired squeak.

One afternoon at 1:05, just as she did every afternoon at 1:05, Maxie moved the bird cage with the yellow bird in it to the front windows. It was shady and cool there now.

The large orange cat moved to the back window and sprawled there, soaking up the sun that matched the color of his fur.

"You're perfectly happy just lying there day after day," Maxie said to the cat. "All you ever want to do is move from one window sill to the other and watch the world go by. You don't need anyone, and no one really needs you. But you don't seem to care." Maxie turned away from the window. "I care," she said sadly. "I'm not a cat. But I might as well be." Maxie felt very tired, and she went to bed.

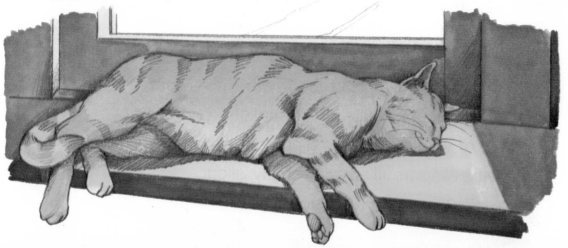

The next morning at seven o'clock the three
shades on Maxie's front windows and the one on
her back window remained down. At 7:10 the
large orange cat was still asleep at the foot of
Maxie's bed. And at 7:30 there were no sweet
warbling sounds. That morning no one heard the
sounds of Maxie's leather slippers on the stairs.
Her teakettle was filled with empty silence.

At nine o'clock the mailman came with the daily mail. He had a seed catalog for Maxie, and he waited for her to come down the stairs. Since she didn't come, and this was most unusual, he decided to deliver the catalog to her door. He climbed the four flights of stairs. He knocked and waited. There was no sign of Maxie.

At 9:03 Mr. Turkle, who lived on the third floor, came hurrying up the stairs. At 9:05 Mr. and Mrs. Moorehouse got there from across the street. At 9:07 Mrs. Trueheart came over from next door. Susie Smith came up at 9:10 with her twin brothers. Five members of the family on the second floor made it up by 9:13. Then came Arthur, the superintendent. By 9:17 there were seventeen people, three dogs, and two cats — all waiting for Maxie to open the door.

And when she didn't, they all went in. They found Maxie in bed. More people came up the stairs, and someone called a doctor. By the time he got there, there were forty-two grown-ups and eleven children in Maxie's small living room.

When the doctor came out of Maxie's bedroom, he shook his head sadly. "Maxie isn't really sick," he said. "She's lonely. She doesn't feel loved. She doesn't feel that anyone needs her."

No one said anything for a minute. Then suddenly Mrs. Trueheart got up and walked right past the doctor and into the bedroom. "Maxie!" she shouted angrily. "You let me down. You and that warbling bird let me down! Every morning when I wake up, I hear that bird. Then it's my job to wake my husband. He has the morning shift at the corner diner, and he's still asleep. Why, there must be at least seventy-five people at that diner right now waiting for their breakfasts. They'll all have to go to work on empty stomachs—all because of you and that yellow bird!"

Everyone else crowded into the bedroom. Maxie
sat up in bed and listened to what they had to say.

"I couldn't go to school this morning," Susie Smith
said. "I missed my bus because I didn't hear your
teakettle whistle."

"The school bus never came this morning," said
Mr. Turkle, who drove the bus. "I didn't wake up
in time. I never heard Sarah Sharpe's footsteps
on my ceiling." Sarah Sharpe lived just above
Mr. Turkle. She always got up when she heard
Maxie's door squeak.

292

Mr. and Mrs. Moorehouse both had very important jobs, but they had missed their train that morning. Their alarm clock was Maxie's window shade. Arthur said he hadn't <u>swept</u> the front steps that morning. He overslept because Maxie didn't ring his bell. He hoped no one would complain.

They all talked about it and decided that there must be about four hundred people who needed Maxie—or who needed someone else who needed Maxie—every morning.

Maxie smiled. She got out of bed and made a pot of tea. In fact she made five pots of tea. Each time the kettle whistled, dogs howled, cats whined, and babies bawled. Maxie listened and thought about how many people were being touched by these sounds—her sounds. By 9:45 that morning Maxie had served tea to everybody, and she was so pleased.

Is That a Fact?

Here are two newspaper stories that tell about the same show. Read them carefully.

Clay School Third-Graders Put On Play

Some girls and boys of the third grade at Clay School gave a one-act play called "Finding Father's Muffler" in the school auditorium last Tuesday afternoon. Sue Conti, Judy Jefferson, and Bob Chen played important roles. Phil Stein played Goober the Dog. Parents, teachers, and the second, third, and fourth grades attended.

Clay School Play a Success

Girls and boys of the third grade at Clay School gave a lively one-act play called "Finding Father's Muffler" in the school auditorium last Tuesday afternoon. Turning in really fine performances were Sue Conti, Judy Jefferson, and Bob Chen. Phil Stein was especially funny as Goober the Dog. Parents, teachers, and the second, third, and fourth grades enjoyed the laugh-packed show very much.

Now answer these questions.

1. Do both stories give the same facts?
   Make lists of the facts in each story to support
   your answer.
2. Which story includes the personal opinions of
   the writer? Make a list of the words and
   phrases in the second story that show the
   writer's personal feelings about the play.
3. Think about the opinions of the writer. Could
   another writer have different opinions? Write a
   sentence or two telling why you think as you do.

In newspapers, magazines, and books you will
read some stories with just facts in them and some
stories that include opinions. And it is important for
you to be able to spot the opinions as you read. If
you can't, without knowing it, you may think that
opinions are facts.

Now look back at "Now You See It, Now You
Don't" and "A Teacher's Teacher" in this book.
Which one has just facts in it? Which one has
opinions, too?

Me and the Ecology Bit

by Joan M. Lexau

Sure is hard to get people to work for ecology.
Everybody is in favor of it, but nobody wants
to do anything about it. At least I'm doing
something, going around telling people what they
should do. But all I get is a lot of back talk.

I have this paper route. Between it and my
homework I hardly have time for playing ball
and stuff.

But anyhow, on Saturdays when I collect the
money for the paper, I put in a good word for
ecology. Like last Saturday morning. It was a
good collecting day. It had just turned spring,
and a lot of people were outside.

I went to Mr. Williams's house. As usual, he tries to pretend he's not home. But I see him burning leaves in the backyard, so he's stuck. He pays me, and I tell him, "You shouldn't burn those leaves. It's bad for the air—bad ecology. You should make a compost pile like we do. Put in the leaves, garbage, and stuff. Good for the garden."

He doesn't agree or hang his head in shame. He says, "That compost pile is your job at home, Jim, isn't it?"

"Yes," I say proudly, which would really shock my dad. He somehow has the idea I hate working with compost. Which I do.

Mr. Williams says, "Well, why don't you take a little more trouble with it—put enough dirt on top of each layer? And turn it over now and then? Then we wouldn't have this nose pollution."

"Huh?" I say. "You mean noise pollution."

"No," he says. "I mean your compost smells up the whole street."

My feelings are hurt, but that doesn't stop me from trying again. I go to collect from Ms. Greene. I have to call her Ms. Greene because if I call her Mrs., she says she doesn't have change to pay me.

She is putting her garbage out for the weekly pickup on Monday. She goes away weekends, so Saturdays and Sundays we have to look at the big plastic garbage bags on her lawn. But I don't say anything about it. I just look at the garbage.

She says to me, "Go pick up that gum wrapper you threw on my lawn. Put it in one of the plastic bags. Didn't anybody teach you not to litter?"

I hold my temper and go pick up my gum wrapper and put it in a bag.

Then she says, "And there's a law in this town about keeping dogs on a leash. So why is yours always all over the place? That dog digs up my garden and messes up my yard, and last weekend Mr. Williams saw it tear open one of my garbage bags."

"Well," I say, but I can't think of anything to go with it. Then I see she is piling newspapers next to her garbage bags.

"Listen, Ms. Greene," I say, "save those papers for the school pickup, and they can be made into new paper. Save aluminum cans, too."

"Like the last school pickup," she asks, "when you said you'd come pick them up, and you never showed up? It's easier to throw them away a few at a time than have a big mess like that."

I get tired trying to get Ms. Greene to do
something about ecology. I go to Mr. Johnson's
house. He makes a run for his car, but I can
run faster than he can.

"Just trying to get to the post office before it
closes," he says, huffing and puffing.

"You got time," I say. "You even got time to
walk. It's only two blocks. You shouldn't take
your car when you don't need to. The walk
would be good exercise and save on gas. And
not pollute. That's ecology."

"How about trees?" he asks me. "Are trees ecology?"

"They sure are," I say. "We had a lot about trees and ecology in school. They make the air better and stuff like that."

"See that tree over there?" he says, pointing to where there isn't any tree.

"I don't see any tree," I tell him.

"Of course not," he says. "And no grass either. Because you made a path there taking a short cut from Mrs. Greene's. There was a little tree just starting to get bigger there until you killed it by trying to jump over it every day. Remember?"

"Oh," I say.

"I drive to the post office to save time," he says. "But now you've made me too late." He goes in the house looking very mad.

Then I remember he hasn't paid me. But I decide to wait until next Saturday. At least I made him not pollute with his car for once.

I don't talk to the rest of my route about ecology. It's very tiring work, this ecology bit.

But when I get home, I see my mother using the <u>electric</u> mixer.

"You should do that with your old egg beater," I point out to her. "Save on electricity. People use too many electric things."

She says in a very cold voice, "So who watches TV twenty-seven hours a day around here? Or is that some other kind of electricity?"

See what I mean? Nobody's willing to do anything about ecology. Except me. And nobody listens to me.

No One Else

by Elaine Laron

Now, someone else can tell you how
To multiply by three.
And someone else can tell you how
To spell SCHENECTADY.
And someone else can tell you how
To ride a two-wheeled bike.
But no one else, no, no one else
Can tell you what to like.

An engineer can tell you how
To run a railroad train.
A map can tell you where to find
The capital of Spain.
A book can tell you all the names
Of every star above.
But no one else, no, no one else
Can tell you who to love.

Your Aunt Louise can tell you how
To plant a pumpkin seed.
Your Cousin Frank can tell you how
To catch a centipede.
Your mom and dad can tell you how
To brush between each meal.
But no one else, no, no one else
Can tell you how to feel.

For how you feel is how you feel
And all the whole world through
No one else, no, no one else
Knows that as well as you!

Glossary

Pronunciation Key

In this Glossary the letters and symbols in parentheses that follow each entry word show you how to pronounce the word. For example, **feath er** (feŦH′ər). The symbols that may puzzle you are shown below. Each symbol is to be pronounced in the way you pronounce the spellings in very black type in the words next to the symbol.

You will see spaces in some of these pronunciations. These spaces show the divisions between syllables.

As part of many of the pronunciations, the mark ′ is placed after a syllable with a primary, or heavy, accent, as in **feath er** (feŦH′ər). The mark ′ is placed after a syllable that has a secondary, or lighter, accent, as in **i mag i na tion** (i maj′ə nā′shən). Sometimes you will see these accent marks in the spaces between syllables.

a **apple, cat**	i **itch, dip**	u **up, cut**
ā **able, day**	ī **ivy, kite**	u̇ **put, cook**
ã **air, pear**		ü **glue, boot**
ä **arm, father**	o **October, hot**	ū **use, music**
	ō **open, go**	
e **elevator, net**	ô **all, saw**	th **thin, both**
ē **each, be**	ôr **order, horse**	ŦH **then, smooth**
ėr **earth, person**		zh **measure, seizure**
	oi **oil, toy**	
	ou **out, cow**	ə **about, occur, until**

Sioux following the pronunciation of an entry word tells you that the entry word is from the language of the Sioux Indians.

Spanish following a pronunciation means the word is from the Spanish language.

ac count ant (ə kount′ənt) a person who takes care of how money is used

ad dress (ə dres′) to write on a letter where it is to be sent; to make a speech to; (ad′res or ə dres′) the place where someone gets mail

ad jec tive (aj′ik tiv) a word that is used to tell something about a noun or pronoun

Af ro (af′rō) a way of wearing the hair short and very curly

a gent (ā′jent) someone who has the right to do something for a club   **secret agent** an agent who works in a hidden way

a gree (ə grē′) to say yes to; to think the same way as someone else

a larm ing (ə lär′ming) suddenly scary or shocking; frightening

a like (ə līk′) like another thing or person

al low ance (ə lou′ns) money someone gets every week or every month

al pha bet i cal or der (al′fə bet′ə kl ôr′dər) listed by letter in the way the letters of the alphabet follow one another

a lu mi num (ə lü′mə nəm) a metal, very light in weight, used for making many things

a maze (ə māz′) to be very surprised; to make someone be very surprised

a muse ment (ə mūz′mənt) something that makes a person laugh or have fun

a part (ə pärt′) away from each other or from others

ap pear (ə pir′) to be seen; to look; to come into sight

ap point ed (ə poin′təd) chosen; set

ap prov al (ə prüv′l) the act of being pleased with

ar e a way (ãr′ē ə wā′) a path between buildings

ar roz con pol lo (är ōs′ kōn poi′yō) *Spanish*, food made with chicken and rice

at tic (at′ik) an open space just under the roof of a house

au di ence (ô′dē əns) a group of people who are together in one place to hear or see a show of some kind

au di to ri um (ô′də tô′rē əm) a large room with a stage and seats for many people where plays and shows are given

a wak en (ə wāk′ən) to wake up

bal ance (bal′əns) equal; to keep steady without falling or dropping

bal co ny (bal′kə nē) a porch that sticks out from an upper floor of a building

base ment (bās′mənt) the lowest floor of a building, partly or all lower than the ground around the building

book let (bùk′lit) a little book, often with a paper cover, that gives special information

bri dle (brī′dl) the straps fitted on an animal's head to lead or control the animal

buf fa lo (buf′l ō) a large animal something like a cow with a big, shaggy head, important to prairie Indians for food and other things

bum ble (bum′bl) to buzz, as a bee does

busi ness like (biz′nis lik′) quick and orderly

Can a da (kan′ə də) the country that borders the United States on the north

Ca na di an (kə nā′dē ən) a person who lives in Canada

ca nar y (kə när′ē) a small, yellow singing bird, often kept as a pet in a cage

cap i tal (kap′ə tl) the city in which the government of a country is located

car ton (kärt′n) a box made of thin cardboard

cas tle (kas′l) a huge building with thick walls and towers, often owned by a king

cat a log (kat′l ôg) a book that is a list of things for sale

cel e brate (sel′ə brāt) to have a good time in order to mark a special happening

cen ti pede (sen′tə pēd) a small, wormlike animal with many pairs of legs

ce re al (sir′ē əl) a breakfast food made from grain

cha hum pi ska (chə hum′pē skä) *Sioux*, sugar made from the sap of trees

char coal (chär′kōl′) pieces of black, burned wood used to help plants drain off water

Chi ca go (shə kô′gō) a large city in Illinois on Lake Michigan

Chip pe wa (chip′ə wä) a tribe of American Indians living in the United States and Canada

choir (kwīr) a group of singers who sing together

cloth ing (klōꝦ′ing) things to wear; clothes

com fort (kum′fərt) to make feel better

com post (kom′pōst) a mixture of leaves, cut grass, and fruit and vegetable waste that is left to rot and then is put into the soil to help plants and gardens grow

com put er (kəm pūt′ər) a machine that can do math and give answers to questions from facts given to it on special cards

Con nect i cut (kə net′ə kət) a state in northeastern United States

con tain er (kən tān′ər) something that holds things, such as a jar, box, or can

---

a **a**pple, ā **a**ble, ã **ai**r, ä **a**rm; e **e**levator, ē **ea**ch, ėr **ear**th; i **i**tch, ī **i**vy;
o **O**ctober, ō **o**pen, ô **a**ll, ôr **or**der; oi **oi**l, ou **ou**t; u **u**p, u̇ **p**ut, ü **gl**ue,
ū **u**se; th **th**in, Ꝧ **th**en, zh mea**s**ure; ə **a**bout, **o**ccur, **u**ntil

cord (kôrd)　a chain that is pulled to turn a light on or off

count (kount)　to name numbers in order to find out how many

cou ple (kup′l)　two of something; a few

cub by hole (kub′ē hōl′)　a small, closed space

cus tom er (kus′təm ər)　someone who buys something

dai sy (dā′zē)　a white flower with a yellow center

da shi ki (də shē′kē)　a loose piece of clothing, like a shirt without buttons, often printed with bright colors

daz zle (daz′l)　a blinding brightness

de cide (di sīd′)　to make up one's mind; to reach an answer

de liv er (di liv′ər)　to carry and give out

dif fi cult (dif′ə kult)　hard; not easy to put up with

dis pose (dis pōz′)　to get rid of; to throw away

dis trict (dis′trikt)　a part of a state or city marked off and organized so that certain work, such as running schools, will be done in the best way

doe (dō)　a deer that can have baby deer

don key (dong′kē)　an animal that looks a little like a horse, but has longer ears and a shorter mane

dou ble (dub′l)　twice; two times as many

driz zle (driz′l)　gentle rain in very small drops

e col o gy (ē kol′ə jē)　the study of how all living things—people, animals, and plants—relate to each other and to the world in which they live

edge (ej)　a line or place where something ends; the sharp outside line of a thing

e lec tric (i lek′trik)　having to do with things run by electricity

e lec tric i ty (i lek′tris′ə tē)　a form of energy that produces light and heat and power to run machines

emp ty (emp′tē)　with nothing or no one in it

en gine (en′jən)　a machine that does work　**fire engine** a large truck that carries firemen and their supplies

en gi neer (en′jə nir′)　a person who runs a railroad engine

en ter tain (en′tər tān′)　to amuse; to please

en trance (en′trəns)　an opening, like a doorway

en ve lope (en′və lōp)　the paper wrapping in which a letter is mailed

er rand (er′ənd)　a short trip to do something

ex cept (ek sept′)　other than; only; but; leaving out

fact (fakt)　something that is known to be true or to have happened　**in fact** really

fan tas tic (fan tas′tik)
amazing; wonderful; very
special or unusual

fa vor (fā′vər)　a liking of;
approval of　　**in favor of**
on the side of; approving

fa vor ite (fā′vər it　or　fāv′rit)
liked better than any other

fierce ly (firs′lē)　angrily;
strongly

fig ure (fig′yər)　to think; a
shape, outline, or form
figure out　to come to
understand by thinking about

fi nal ly (fī′nl ē)　at the end;
at last

fiz zle (fiz′l)　a hissing or
sputtering

flute (flüt)　a long, slim pipe on
which music can be made by
blowing across a hole at one
end and blocking and
unblocking holes in it

gal lop (gal′əp)　to run very
fast

ga rage (gə räzh′　or　gə räj′)
a building where cars are kept

gar bage (gär′bij)　scraps of
food and other things to be
thrown away

germs (jėrmz)　animals or
plants that can cause sickness
and are too little to be seen

gi ant (jī′ənt)　a make-believe
person that looks like a human
being but is much stronger and
larger than a real person; huge

glance (glans)　a quick look

glide (glīd)　to move in a
smooth and easy way

glis ten (glis′n)　to shine,
sparkle, or glitter

glos sa ry (glos′ə rē)　a list of
words that tells how to say
each word and what it means
as it is used in the book

gob ble (gob′l)　to eat fast and
in big bites

gold (gōld)　coins or money
made of a costly metal that is
shiny and bright yellow; bright
yellow

goof (güf)　to do fun things that
one likes to do; to waste time

grace (grās)　beauty of form,
movement, or behavior

grav el (grav′l)　little pieces of
rocks larger than sand

grav i ty (grav′ə tē)　the force
that pulls things toward the
center of the earth

guin ea pig (gin′ē　pig) a
small, short-eared,
furry animal, often
kept as a pet

hand some (han′səm)　good-
looking

hel i cop ter (hel′ə kop′tər)
an aircraft that has propellers
on top

heart (härt)　one's feelings or
mind; center or middle

hel che tu al oh (hel′chə tü
el ō′)　*Sioux,* it is right; it is
true

---

a **a**pple, ā **a**ble, ã **air**, ä **a**rm; e **e**levator, ē **ea**ch, ėr **ear**th; i **i**tch, ī **i**vy;
o **O**ctober, ō **o**pen, ô **a**ll, ôr **or**der; oi **oi**l, ou **ou**t; u **u**p, u̇ **pu**t, ü **g**l**ue**,
ū **use**; th **th**in, ₮H **th**en, zh mea**s**ure; ə **a**bout, **o**ccur, **u**ntil

hey-a-hey (hā′ə hā) sounds made to show surprise, happiness, or a feeling of being pleased

hind (hīnd) back; rear

home stead er (hōm′sted ər) someone who settled on new farmland given to him or her by the United States

Il li nois (il′ə noi′) a state in the northern middle part of the United States

In di an (in′dē ən) people who were living in America long before settlers came from Europe

In di an O cean (in′dē ən ō′shən) a large body of water south of Asia and east of Africa

in stant (in′stənt) the very same time

in vis i ble (in viz′ ə bl) unseen; that cannot be seen

in vi ta tion (in və tā′shən) a note asking someone to come somewhere or to do something

i ron work er (ī′ərn wėr′kər) someone who builds the steel frames of bridges and very tall buildings

i vy (ī′vē) a plant with smooth, shiny green leaves that clings to something like a fence or a wall as it grows

Jap a nese (jap′ə nēz′) people of Japan

Ju pi ter (jü′pə tər) the largest planet, about 318 times as big as Earth

Ken tuck y (kən tuk′ē) a southern state of the United States

ki mo no (kə mō′nə) a loose outer piece of clothing something like a robe

lim it (lim′it) the most that something can hold

Lon don (lun′dən) a very large city in England

lum ber jack (lum′bər jak′) someone who cuts down trees and moves them to mills where they are cut up

Mars (märz) the planet nearest to Earth, about ten times smaller than Earth

may or (mā′ər) the main officer of a city or town

mead ow (med′ō) a field of grassy land

med i cine (med′ə sən) something a sick person or animal takes to get better

mes sage (mes′ij) written words sent from one person to another; the meaning

mis er a ble (miz′ər ə bl) very unhappy; sad

Mo hawk (mō′hôk) a tribe of American Indians living in the north part of New York state and in Canada; a member of that tribe

mo las ses (mə las′iz) a very thick, sweet syrup

mo ment (mō′mənt) a very short time; less than a minute

Mont re al (mont′rē ôl′) the largest city in Canada

Ms. (miz)   a formal title given to all women, as "Mr." is used for all men

mys ter y (mis′tər ē or mis′trē)   something that is unknown; something that is not understood

ni ños (nē′nyōs)   *Spanish*, children

no tice (nō′tis)   to see; to see and understand

nurse (nėrs)   a person who takes care of sick people

of fice (ôf′is)   a place where some kinds of work are done

post office   a place where stamps are sold and letters and packages are mailed

of fi cial (ə fish′əl)   real; right; agreed to by important people

op er ate (op′ər āt)   to do something to an animal, usually by a doctor using special tools, in order to fix something wrong; to make something work or run

o pin ion (ə pin′yən)   a belief about something not based on proof or facts

or der (ôr′dər)   the way one thing follows another; the way things are done, one after the other   **to come to order**   to begin a meeting; to get to work

o rig i nal (ə rij′ə nl) belonging to or coming from the first or earliest

owe (ō)   to have to pay or repay

pail (pāl)   a round container, usually with a handle, used for carrying or holding things

pa ja mas (pə jä′məz or pə jam′əz)   clothes worn to sleep in

Pa pa go (pä′pä gō)   a tribe of American Indians living in Arizona

pa rade (pə rād′)   a march, usually with music

pa tient (pā′shənt)   an animal or person who is being taken care of by a doctor

paw (pô)   the foot of an animal that has claws

per form ance (pər fôr′məns) an act done in public

per son al (pėr′sn l) belonging to only one person

phrase (frāz)   a group of words that is less than a sentence

pi geon (pij′ən)   a kind of bird that often lives in cities

plan et (plan′it)   one of the bodies that moves around the sun, such as Earth, Jupiter, and Mars

plead (plēd)   to ask with strong feeling; to beg

po lite ly (pə līt′lē)   with good manners

---

a **a**pple, ā **a**ble, ã **air**, ä **a**rm; e **e**levator, ē **ea**ch, ėr **ear**th; i **i**tch, ī **i**vy; o **O**ctober, ō **o**pen, ô **a**ll, ôr **or**der; oi **oi**l, ou **ou**t; u **u**p, u̇ **pu**t, ü **glu**e, ū **u**se; th **th**in, ŦH **th**en, zh mea**s**ure; ə **a**bout, **o**ccur, **u**ntil

pol lu tion (pə lü′shən) the dirtying or destroying of the air, soil, or water

porch (pôrch) an open or covered platform attached to the outside of a house

post (pōst) the mail   **post card** a card to send in the mail, with a place to write a message on one side and a place to write an address on the other side

po ta to (pə tā′tō) a plant that people and some animals eat

prai rie (prãr′ē) lots of flat land, covered with grass, but few trees

pre fix (prē′fiks) a group of letters standing for sounds and added to the beginning of some words to change the meaning of those words, such as "un-" in "unhappy"

prick ly (prik′lē) sharp and stinging

prin ci pal (prin′sə pl) a person who is the head of a school

puz zle (puz′l) to be mixed up about something; to not be able to find the answer right away

qui et (kwī′ət) still; with little or no noise

re al ize (rē′əl īz) to under-stand clearly; to know

rear (rir) to stand up on the back legs only

rec i pe (res′ə pē) directions for making something to eat

rein (rān) a long, thin strap hooked at one end to other straps that are around an animal's head, and held at the other end by someone leading or steering the animal

re main (ri mān′) to stay on in a place

re pairs (ri pãrz′) work done on things that need fixing

re peat (ri pēt′) to say again

re ply (ri plī′) to answer

res er va tion (rez′ər vā′shən) land owned by the United States for Indians to live on

res tau rant (res′tə rənt) a place where people pay for a meal that is cooked and served to them

re turn (ri tėrn′) to come back or go back to a place left for a time

rhythm (riŦH′əm) a movement with a repeated beat

romp (romp) to play in a rough way, rushing and tumbling

rose hip tea (rōz hip tē) a kind of tea, used sometimes long ago to treat sick people, made from a dried part of the rose flower called the hip

rub ble (rub′l) broken stones, bricks, and junk left after a building has been torn down

ru ined (rü′ənd) spoiled; fallen down or apart

sail or (sāl′ər) someone who works on a ship or boat

Sche nec ta dy (skə nek′- tə dē) a city in the east part of New York state

scram ble (skram′bl) to mix together, such as cooked eggs with the white and yellow parts mixed; to climb or crawl

search (sėrch) to look over carefully; to try to find by looking; to look carefully for something lost or hidden

sec ond (sek′ənd) coming after the first; another

sec ond (sek′ənd) a very little bit of time, less than a minute

seize (sēz) to grab; to take hold of suddenly

self-con fi dence (sėlf′kon′fə- dəns) a person's own belief and trust in what he or she is and what he or she can do

sep a rate (sep′ə rit) own; apart from the others

sew er (sü′ər) a pipe that goes under the ground to carry away water and waste

sheep ish (shēp′ish) feeling dumb and foolish

she o (shē′ō) *Sioux*, prairie hen

short stop (shôrt′ stop′) the baseball player who plays between second base and third base

shov el (shuv′l) a tool used to lift and throw dirt

shrill (shril) high and sharp in sound

shrub (shrub) a bush

sign (sīn) a hint or trace; to write one's own name

si lent (sī′lənt) quiet; making no sound or noise

sin gle (sing′gl) one

Sioux (sü) a tribe of American Indians living in the central part of the United States; the language of that tribe; a member of that tribe

slain (slān) killed; murdered

South Da ko ta (south də kō′tə) a state in the middle of the United States

spa ghet ti (spə get′ē) a food made by mixing tomato sauce with cooked spaghetti, which are long, skinny noodles

Spain (spān) a country in southwest Europe, between the Mediterranean Sea and the Atlantic Ocean

spar row (spar′ō) a small brown or gray bird

spec ta tor (spek′tā tər) someone who watches something happening without taking part in it

sprawl (sprôl) to lie down with the legs thrown out

spread (spred) to become widely known; to stretch out

stall (stôl) a small room, big enough for only one animal, in a barn

steer ing (stir′ing) leading or guiding the way

---

a **a**pple, ā **a**ble, ã **air**, ä **a**rm; e **e**levator, ē **ea**ch, ėr **ear**th; i **i**tch, ī **i**vy; o O**c**tober, ō **o**pen, ô **a**ll, ôr **or**der; oi **oi**l, ou **ou**t; u **u**p, u̇ **pu**t, ü **glue**, ū **use**; th **thi**n, ŦH **the**n, zh mea**s**ure; ə **a**bout, **o**ccur, **u**ntil

St. Law rence Riv er (sānt lô′rəns riv′ər) a long river flowing between the United States and Canada, east of the Great Lakes

strange (strānj) odd; very different; not known, seen, or heard before

sub way (sub′wā′) a train that runs under the ground

suf fix (suf′iks) a special ending added to some words that shows how those words are used in a sentence — as a noun or verb and so on, such as "-ness" in "happiness"

suit (süt) a set of clothes

su per in ten dent (sü′prin-tend′nt or sü′pər in tend′nt) a person who directs or manages

sup port (sə pôrt′) to help prove; to back up

sur pass (sər pas′) to do better than; to be greater than

Swed ish (swēd′ish) having to do with the country of Sweden, its language, or its people

swirl y (swėrl′ē) dizzy; sick from moving; seasick

sym bol (sim′bl) something that stands for or takes the place of something else

ta co (tä′kō) a thin, flat, round corn cake bent in half and filled with chopped meat, cheese, and some vegetables, served hot

tal ent (tal′ənt) a special natural ability

tam bou rine (tam′bə rēn′) a small drum with metal circles in its sides that make noise when the drum is hit or shaken

tea ket tle (tē′ket′l) a metal container with a spout, used for boiling water to make tea

te pee (tē′pē) a kind of tent that some Indian tribes used to sleep in when they traveled

ter rar i um (tə rãr′ē əm) a small indoor garden growing in a glass jar or bowl

ter ri fied (ter′ə fīd) very frightened; really scared

thread (thred) to put sewing thread through the eye of a needle

tim id (tim′id) shy; not sure

to mor row (tə môr′ō) the day after today

trav el er (trav′l ər) someone who goes from one place to another

treas ure (trezh′ər) something that is very important to someone

trou sers (trou′zərz) a pair of long pants; slacks

tug (tug) a small boat that pulls and pushes larger boats and ships; to pull

tune (tün or tūn) a song

tur nip (tėr′nəp) a plant with a big, round root good to eat

twice (twīs) two times as much or as great

twirl (twėrl) to turn around very fast; to spin

u ni verse (ū′nə vėrs) every-thing that is, Earth and all the other planets

u su al (ū′zhu̇ əl) in the same way; as always

va ca tion (vā kā′shən) a time of fun and rest when a person is not working

vet er i nar i an (vet′ər ə-nãr′ē ən) a doctor who takes care of animals

vis it (viz′it) to go or to come to see someone or something; a stay as a guest

vol un teer (vol′ən tir′) made of people who do a job for free

wan der (won′dər) to move here and there without any special direction

wart hog (wôrt hog) a wild pig that has large tusks and has lumps on its face

Was i chus (wäsh ē′chüs) *Sioux*, white people

whole (hōl) all of something

wind mill (wind′mil) a pump run by the wind that brings water up out of the ground

win dow pane (win′dō pān′) the piece of glass in a window

with drew (wiŦH drü′) took out or away

wolf (wu̇lf) an animal that looks something like a dog, but that can't be made into a pet

Character and Biographical Names

An a (än′ə)
Bun yan, Paul (bun′yən, pôl)
Car los (kär′lōs)
Char ley (chär′lē)
Char lotte (shär′lət)
Cle o (klē′ō)
Con ti (kont′ē)
Cos tan za (kos ton′zə)
Fli er (flī′ər)
Gar cí a (gär sē′ə)
Juan (hwän)
Lau ro (lôr′ō)
Ma má (mə mä′)
Man uel a (män wel′ə)
Mi e ko (mi e kō)
Mi guel (mē gel′)
Mit ya (mit′yə)

Ni na (nē′nə)
Pa pa (pä′pə)
Pa pá (pə pä′)
Pe dro (pā′drō)
Ri car do (ri kär′dō)
Ro dri guez (rō drē′gəz)
Sak a mo to (sä kä mō tō)
Stein (stīn)
Ta ku (tä kü)
Tor toise (tôr′təs)
Tur kle (tėr′kl)
Wash ing ton, Gen er al George (wosh′ing tən, jen′ər əl jôrj)
Wick, Tem pe (wik, tem pē′)
Yo lan da (yō län′də)
Yu ri (yu̇r ē)

a apple, ā able, ã air, ä arm; e elevator, ē each, ėr earth; i itch, ī ivy;
o October, ō open, ô all, ôr order; oi oil, ou out; u up, u̇ put, ü glue,
ū use; th thin, ŦH then, zh measure; ə about, occur, until